CYBERWATCH 101

THE ART OF CYBER DEFENSE AND INFRASTRUCTURE SECURITY

4 BOOKS IN 1

BOOK 1
CYBERWATCH: A BEGINNER'S GUIDE TO DIGITAL SECURITY

BOOK 2
MASTERING CYBERWATCH: ADVANCED TECHNIQUES FOR CYBERSECURITY PROFESSIONALS

BOOK 3
CYBERWATCH CHRONICLES: FROM NOVICE TO NINJA IN CYBER DEFENSE

BOOK 4
CYBERWATCH UNLEASHED: EXPERT STRATEGIES FOR SAFEGUARDING YOUR DIGITAL WORLD

ROB BOTWRIGHT

Published by Rob Botwright
Library of Congress Cataloging-in-Publication Data
ISBN 978-1-83938-605-3
Cover design by Rizzo

Disclaimer

The contents of this book are based on extensive research and the best available historical sources. However, the author and publisher make no claims, promises, or guarantees about the accuracy, completeness, or adequacy of the information contained herein. The information in this book is provided on an "as is" basis, and the author and publisher disclaim any and all liability for any errors, omissions, or inaccuracies in the information or for any actions taken in reliance on such information. The opinions and views expressed in this book are those of the author and do not necessarily reflect the official policy or position of any organization or individual mentioned in this book. Any reference to specific people, places, or events is intended only to provide historical context and is not intended to defame or malign any group, individual, or entity. The information in this book is intended for educational and entertainment purposes only. It is not intended to be a substitute for professional advice or judgment. Readers are encouraged to conduct their own research and to seek professional advice where appropriate. Every effort has been made to obtain necessary permissions and acknowledgments for all images and other copyrighted material used in this book. Any errors or omissions in this regard are unintentional, and the author and publisher will correct them in future editions.

BOOK 1 - CYBERWATCH: A BEGINNER'S GUIDE TO DIGITAL SECURITY

BOOK 2 - MASTERING CYBERWATCH: ADVANCED TECHNIQUES FOR CYBERSECURITY PROFESSIONALS

BOOK 3 - CYBERWATCH CHRONICLES: FROM NOVICE TO NINJA IN CYBER DEFENSE

BOOK 4 - CYBERWATCH UNLEASHED: EXPERT STRATEGIES FOR SAFEGUARDING YOUR DIGITAL WORLD

Introduction

In our rapidly evolving digital age, the importance of cybersecurity has never been more critical. The digital landscape is a realm of boundless opportunities and innovation, but it also presents an ever-growing array of threats and vulnerabilities. In response to this dynamic challenge, we present "CYBERWATCH 101: The Art of Cyber Defense and Infrastructure Security" – a comprehensive book bundle that equips you with the knowledge and skills to protect your digital world.

This bundle comprises four meticulously crafted books, each tailored to a specific level of expertise, from beginners to seasoned professionals. Together, they form a comprehensive roadmap for navigating the complex terrain of cybersecurity, empowering you to become a guardian of your digital existence.

"BOOK 1 - CYBERWATCH: A BEGINNER'S GUIDE TO DIGITAL SECURITY" serves as your initial stepping stone into the world of cybersecurity. It lays the groundwork, helping you understand the fundamental concepts, threats, and vulnerabilities that permeate the digital realm. With this solid foundation, you will be prepared to build a resilient defense against the ever-evolving threats to your digital life.

"BOOK 2 - MASTERING CYBERWATCH: ADVANCED TECHNIQUES FOR CYBERSECURITY PROFESSIONALS" takes you on a deep dive into the realm of advanced cybersecurity techniques. Whether you are an aspiring cybersecurity professional or an experienced expert, this book equips you with the tools, tactics, and strategies needed to master the art of cyber defense. From penetration testing to advanced encryption, you will gain the expertise necessary to thwart even the most sophisticated cyber threats.

"BOOK 3 - CYBERWATCH CHRONICLES: FROM NOVICE TO NINJA IN CYBER DEFENSE" chronicles your transformation from a novice to a cybersecurity ninja. This book showcases the evolution of your skills as you delve into network security, incident response, ethical hacking, and more. By the end of this journey, you will have honed your abilities to become a formidable guardian of digital security.

"BOOK 4 - CYBERWATCH UNLEASHED: EXPERT STRATEGIES FOR SAFEGUARDING YOUR DIGITAL WORLD" takes you into the realm of cybersecurity expertise. As an expert, you will explore advanced cryptographic protocols, secure IoT devices, and navigate the intricate legal and ethical aspects of cybersecurity. Armed with these expert strategies, you will be prepared to safeguard your digital world against the most formidable threats.

In "CYBERWATCH 101," we embark on a transformative journey through the world of cybersecurity. Whether you are a beginner taking your first steps, a professional seeking advanced knowledge, or an expert refining your skills, this bundle is your comprehensive guide to mastering the art of cyber defense and infrastructure security.

Your digital world is a valuable asset, and safeguarding it is a responsibility that requires continuous learning and adaptation. Join us in this journey as we equip you with the knowledge and skills to protect your digital future in the ever-evolving cyber landscape. Welcome to "CYBERWATCH 101: The Art of Cyber Defense and Infrastructure Security."

BOOK 1
CYBERWATCH
A BEGINNER'S GUIDE TO DIGITAL SECURITY
ROB BOTWRIGHT

Chapter 1: Understanding the Digital Landscape

The story of the internet begins in the early days of computer networking, a time when the concept of a global information network was just a distant dream. In the 1960s, researchers and scientists were already envisioning a way to connect computers across vast distances to share information and resources. The idea was to create a decentralized network that could survive even in the face of a nuclear attack, ensuring that critical information could still be exchanged. This vision gave birth to ARPANET, the precursor to the modern internet, which was funded by the U.S. Department of Defense's Advanced Research Projects Agency, or ARPA.

The first message ever sent over ARPANET was a simple "LOGIN" command, sent from one computer at the University of California, Los Angeles, to another at the Stanford Research Institute on October 29, 1969. This momentous event marked the beginning of a revolution that would transform the way people communicated, worked, and lived. ARPANET quickly grew, connecting more and more universities and research institutions across the United States.

In the 1970s, the development of the Transmission Control Protocol (TCP) and Internet Protocol (IP) laid the foundation for the modern internet. These protocols allowed different networks to communicate with each other, creating a unified network of networks, which we now know as the internet. The creation of email in the early 1970s and the adoption of the "@" symbol as the separator in email addresses were significant milestones that helped define the internet's functionality.

The 1980s saw the introduction of domain names, which made it easier for people to access websites and services. The World Wide Web, invented by Tim Berners-Lee in 1989, provided a graphical interface for accessing information on the internet, making it accessible to a broader audience. The introduction of the first web browser, Mosaic, in 1993 further accelerated the web's growth and popularity.

The 1990s witnessed a rapid expansion of the internet, as businesses and individuals began to recognize its potential. The dot-com bubble emerged, with numerous startups and companies racing to establish an online presence. The proliferation of websites, e-commerce platforms, and online services transformed the way people shopped, communicated, and conducted business.

The turn of the century brought about significant advancements in internet technology. The launch of broadband internet made it possible for users to access high-speed connections, paving the way for streaming media, online gaming, and video conferencing. Social media platforms like Facebook, Twitter, and YouTube emerged, reshaping how people interacted and shared information.

Mobile internet access became mainstream with the advent of smartphones, enabling people to access the internet on the go. The rise of mobile apps added a new dimension to the internet experience, offering countless services and utilities at users' fingertips. The introduction of 3G, 4G, and eventually 5G networks further improved mobile internet speeds and capabilities.

The internet has not only transformed communication and entertainment but has also revolutionized industries such as education, healthcare, and finance. Online education platforms offer access to a wealth of educational resources, while telemedicine allows patients to consult with healthcare professionals remotely. Online banking and digital payment systems have made financial transactions more accessible and convenient.

However, the internet's rapid growth has also raised concerns about privacy, security, and digital divides. Cybersecurity threats, such as hacking and data breaches, have become more prevalent, necessitating stronger measures to protect sensitive information. Issues related to online privacy and the collection of user data have led to debates and discussions about digital rights and regulations.

The digital divide remains a challenge, with disparities in internet access and digital literacy persisting among different populations and regions. Bridging this divide is essential to ensure that everyone can fully participate in the digital age and access the opportunities the internet offers.

As we look to the future, the internet continues to evolve. Emerging technologies like artificial intelligence, the Internet of Things (IoT), and blockchain are poised to shape the next phase of the internet's development. These technologies have the potential to further streamline and enhance various aspects of our lives, from automation and smart homes to secure digital identities and decentralized systems.

The internet has come a long way from its humble beginnings as ARPANET. It has grown into a global phenomenon that connects billions of people, devices, and information sources. Its impact on society, culture, and the economy is immeasurable, and its potential for innovation and transformation remains boundless.

As we navigate the ever-changing landscape of the internet, it is essential to remain vigilant, informed, and responsible users. By understanding its history, appreciating its significance, and addressing its challenges, we can make the most of this powerful tool while ensuring a safe and inclusive digital future.

The evolution of the digital world has been a remarkable journey, one that has transformed nearly every aspect of our lives. From the advent of personal computers to the proliferation of smartphones and the rise of the internet, technology has reshaped how we work, communicate, and connect with one another. The story of this transformation is a complex tapestry of innovation, entrepreneurship, and societal change that spans decades.

In the early 1970s, the introduction of the microprocessor paved the way for the development of personal computers, making computing power accessible to individuals and small businesses. This marked the beginning of a revolution that would democratize information and computing, allowing people to harness the power of technology in their everyday lives.

The 1980s saw the emergence of the graphical user interface (GUI), which made computers more user-friendly and intuitive. Apple's Macintosh and Microsoft's Windows operating systems played pivotal roles in popularizing the GUI and setting the stage for the computer revolution. Soon, desktop publishing, word processing, and spreadsheet software became indispensable tools for businesses and individuals alike.

The 1990s witnessed the rapid growth of the internet, a network of networks that connected people and information across the globe. The World Wide Web, invented by Tim Berners-Lee, provided a user-friendly interface for accessing information on the internet. With the introduction of web browsers like Netscape Navigator and Internet Explorer, the web became a dynamic platform for communication and commerce.

E-commerce exploded in the late 1990s with the dot-com boom, as countless startups and businesses rushed to establish an online presence. Companies like Amazon and eBay transformed the way people shopped, while search engines like Google revolutionized information retrieval. The internet's potential as a platform for innovation and entrepreneurship became evident.

The early 2000s brought the rise of mobile technology, with the introduction of smartphones that combined the capabilities of phones, cameras, and personal organizers. Apple's iPhone, released in 2007, redefined the smartphone landscape and introduced the concept of mobile apps, creating a new ecosystem for software development and distribution.

Social media platforms like Facebook, Twitter, and YouTube gained prominence, enabling people to connect, share, and communicate with each other on a global scale. Social media revolutionized the way we interacted, with profound implications for communication, marketing, and even political discourse.

The cloud computing revolution of the 2010s changed how businesses and individuals stored and accessed data. Cloud services provided scalable and flexible solutions for data storage and application hosting, reducing the reliance on local hardware and infrastructure. This shift allowed for greater mobility and collaboration, as users could access their data and applications from anywhere with an internet connection.

Artificial intelligence (AI) and machine learning emerged as transformative technologies, powering intelligent algorithms that could analyze vast amounts of data and make predictions and recommendations. AI applications ranged from virtual assistants and chatbots to self-driving cars and advanced healthcare diagnostics.

Blockchain technology, initially developed for cryptocurrencies like Bitcoin, gained attention for its potential to revolutionize industries beyond finance. Its decentralized and transparent ledger system offered new possibilities for secure and verifiable transactions, supply chain management, and digital identity verification.

The Internet of Things (IoT) brought connectivity to everyday objects, from smart thermostats and wearables to industrial sensors and autonomous vehicles. The ability to collect and analyze data from interconnected devices promised to enhance efficiency and convenience in various sectors.

As the digital world continued to evolve, discussions about ethics, privacy, and cybersecurity became increasingly important. Debates surrounding data privacy, surveillance, and the responsible use of technology raised complex ethical questions that required thoughtful consideration.

The COVID-19 pandemic accelerated digital transformation across industries, with remote work, telemedicine, and e-commerce becoming essential for continuity. It underscored the critical role of technology in addressing global challenges and reshaping the way we live and work.

Looking ahead, the digital world continues to hold immense promise and potential. Innovations in quantum computing, renewable energy, and space exploration hint at exciting possibilities on the horizon. The journey of shaping the modern digital world is ongoing, driven by human ingenuity, creativity, and the pursuit of a better future.

As we navigate this ever-changing landscape, it is essential to approach technology with a sense of responsibility and ethical awareness. By harnessing the power of technology while respecting individual rights and societal values, we can ensure that the digital world continues to enrich our lives and enhance our collective progress.

Chapter 2: The Fundamentals of Cyber Threats

Cyber threats represent a diverse and constantly evolving landscape of risks and vulnerabilities that pose significant challenges to individuals, organizations, and society as a whole. These threats can take various forms, each with its own distinct characteristics and potential impact. Understanding the categories of cyber threats is essential for comprehending the breadth and depth of the challenges we face in the digital age.

One of the most common categories of cyber threats is malware, which encompasses a wide range of malicious software designed to compromise and gain unauthorized access to computer systems and data. Malware includes viruses, worms, Trojans, spyware, and ransomware, all of which can infiltrate systems and cause extensive damage.

Phishing attacks represent another prevalent category of cyber threats. Phishing involves the use of deceptive emails, messages, or websites to trick individuals into revealing sensitive information, such as login credentials or financial details. These attacks often exploit human psychology and trust to manipulate victims.

Distributed Denial of Service (DDoS) attacks constitute a category of threats that aim to overwhelm a target's network or website with an excessive volume of traffic, rendering it inaccessible to legitimate users. Cybercriminals orchestrate DDoS attacks using botnets, networks of compromised devices, to amplify the impact.

Social engineering attacks leverage psychological manipulation to deceive individuals or gain unauthorized access to systems. Techniques such as pretexting, baiting, and tailgating exploit human vulnerabilities to extract information or breach security measures.

Another category of cyber threats is insider threats, which originate from individuals within an organization who misuse their access privileges or intentionally compromise security. Insider threats can result from employees with malicious intent, negligent actions, or unintentional mistakes.

Zero-day vulnerabilities are a category of threats related to previously unknown security flaws in software or hardware. Cybercriminals exploit these vulnerabilities before developers have the chance to release patches or updates, making them particularly dangerous.

Supply chain attacks target the weak points in a network by compromising trusted suppliers or vendors. By infiltrating a trusted source, cybercriminals can introduce malware or compromise the integrity of products or services.

State-sponsored cyberattacks represent a category of threats driven by nation-states or government entities with the intent of espionage, disruption, or theft of sensitive information. These attacks can have significant geopolitical implications.

Cyber-espionage, often associated with advanced persistent threats (APTs), is a category of threats aimed at infiltrating organizations, governments, or institutions to gather intelligence or conduct covert operations over an extended period.

Data breaches constitute a category of threats wherein unauthorized parties gain access to sensitive data, potentially leading to the exposure of personal information, financial records, or intellectual property. Data breaches can have severe consequences for individuals and organizations.

Ransomware attacks, a subset of malware threats, involve encrypting a victim's data and demanding a ransom for its release. These attacks have become increasingly common and financially motivated, targeting individuals and businesses alike.

Cyber threats related to critical infrastructure represent a category that poses risks to essential systems, such as energy grids, water supplies, and transportation networks. A breach in critical infrastructure can have widespread and devastating consequences.

IoT (Internet of Things) threats are a category of risks associated with the proliferation of connected devices. Insecure IoT devices can be exploited by cybercriminals to gain access to networks or launch attacks.

Cryptojacking is a category of threats involving the unauthorized use of a victim's computing resources to mine cryptocurrencies. Cybercriminals exploit vulnerabilities to hijack devices and harness their processing power for mining.

Financial cyber threats encompass various attacks targeting financial institutions, payment systems, and individuals' financial assets. These threats include banking Trojans, carding, and ATM attacks.

The category of cyber threats is not static but continuously evolving. New forms of threats and attack techniques emerge as technology advances, creating an ongoing challenge for cybersecurity professionals and organizations worldwide. Staying informed and proactive in addressing these threats is crucial to maintaining digital security and resilience in an interconnected world.

Assessing vulnerabilities and risks is a fundamental aspect of cybersecurity, providing a critical foundation for the development of effective security strategies. Vulnerabilities refer to weaknesses or flaws in a system's design, implementation, or configuration that can be exploited by attackers to compromise the system's integrity, availability, or confidentiality. These vulnerabilities can exist in hardware, software, network configurations, or even human processes and behaviors.

Identifying vulnerabilities involves a thorough examination of all aspects of an organization's digital ecosystem, from its software and hardware to its policies and procedures.

Vulnerability assessments typically involve both automated scanning tools and manual inspection to uncover potential weaknesses.

Once vulnerabilities are identified, the next step is risk assessment, which involves evaluating the potential impact of an exploited vulnerability and the likelihood of it occurring. Risk assessment helps organizations prioritize their efforts by focusing on vulnerabilities that pose the greatest threats.

Risk assessment considers factors such as the value of the asset at risk, the potential harm that could result from an attack, the likelihood of an attack occurring, and the effectiveness of existing security controls. By combining these factors, organizations can assign a risk score to each vulnerability and prioritize mitigation efforts accordingly.

It's important to note that not all vulnerabilities pose the same level of risk. Some vulnerabilities may have a low impact or be highly unlikely to be exploited, while others may have a significant impact and a higher likelihood of being targeted by attackers.

Organizations must strike a balance between the resources they invest in mitigating vulnerabilities and the level of risk they are willing to accept. This balance can vary depending on factors such as an organization's industry, regulatory requirements, and risk tolerance.

To assess vulnerabilities and risks effectively, organizations often conduct regular security assessments and penetration testing. Penetration testing involves simulating real-world attacks to identify vulnerabilities that may not be apparent through automated scans or static analysis. These tests provide valuable insights into an organization's security posture and help uncover potential weaknesses that need to be addressed.

In addition to internal assessments, organizations should also consider external factors that can introduce vulnerabilities and risks. Third-party vendors, partners, and suppliers may introduce vulnerabilities through the products or services they provide, making it crucial to assess the security practices of these external entities.

The evolving threat landscape requires continuous monitoring and assessment of vulnerabilities and risks. New vulnerabilities are discovered regularly, and cyber threats are constantly evolving. Organizations must stay vigilant and adapt their security strategies accordingly.

One critical aspect of risk assessment is understanding the potential consequences of a security breach. The impact of a data breach or cyberattack can be far-reaching, encompassing financial losses, reputational damage, legal liabilities, and regulatory fines. These consequences can be severe and long-lasting, making risk assessment an essential element of cybersecurity planning.

Risk assessment is not a one-time activity; it is an ongoing process that should be integrated into an organization's overall risk management framework. As technology and business environments change, so do the associated risks and vulnerabilities. Regular assessments ensure that security measures remain effective and aligned with the evolving threat landscape.

In addition to assessing vulnerabilities and risks, organizations must also consider the human element of cybersecurity. Employee training and awareness programs play a crucial role in reducing the likelihood of security incidents caused by human error or negligence.

Phishing attacks, for example, often exploit human vulnerabilities by tricking individuals into disclosing sensitive information or clicking on malicious links. Training programs can educate employees on recognizing and responding to phishing attempts, reducing the risk of falling victim to such attacks.

Furthermore, organizations should implement strong access controls and authentication mechanisms to limit the potential impact of security breaches. Multi-factor authentication (MFA) is a powerful tool that adds an extra layer of security by requiring users to provide multiple forms of verification before gaining access to sensitive systems or data.

Regularly patching and updating software and systems is another critical aspect of vulnerability management. Software vendors release patches to address known vulnerabilities, and failing to apply these patches promptly can leave systems exposed to exploitation.

In summary, assessing vulnerabilities and risks is a foundational step in effective cybersecurity. It involves identifying weaknesses, evaluating their potential impact and likelihood, and prioritizing mitigation efforts. Ongoing assessments and monitoring are essential to stay ahead of evolving threats and maintain a strong security posture. Additionally, organizations must address the human element of cybersecurity through training, access controls, and regular software updates to reduce vulnerabilities and mitigate risks effectively.

Chapter 3: Building a Strong Password Fortress

Crafting strong and unique passwords is a critical aspect of cybersecurity, as passwords serve as the first line of defense against unauthorized access to accounts and sensitive information. Passwords play a vital role in protecting personal data, financial assets, and digital identities in an increasingly interconnected world.

A strong password is one that is difficult for attackers to guess or crack through brute force methods. Weak passwords, such as "123456" or "password," are easily guessable and should be avoided at all costs.

To craft a strong password, consider using a combination of uppercase and lowercase letters, numbers, and special characters. This mix of character types increases the complexity of the password and makes it more resistant to automated attacks.

It's essential to choose a password that is sufficiently long to provide a robust defense against attackers. Longer passwords are generally more secure than shorter ones because they have a larger number of possible combinations.

Avoid using easily guessable information, such as common words, phrases, or patterns like "qwerty" or "abcdef." Attackers often employ dictionary attacks and password-cracking tools that can quickly guess passwords based on known words or patterns.

To create a unique password, refrain from using the same password for multiple accounts or services. Reusing passwords increases the risk of a security breach, as a compromised password from one account can potentially grant access to other accounts.

Consider using a passphrase, which is a sequence of random words or a sentence. Passphrases are easier to remember than complex strings of characters and can be highly secure if chosen carefully.

Avoid using personal information in your passwords, such as birthdays, names of family members, or easily discoverable details. Attackers may attempt to guess passwords using information readily available on social media or public records.

Regularly changing passwords is a good practice to minimize the risk of unauthorized access, especially for accounts that contain sensitive or confidential information. However, it's essential to strike a balance between changing passwords regularly and ensuring they remain strong and unique.

Consider using a reputable password manager to generate, store, and manage your passwords securely. Password managers can generate complex and unique passwords for each of your accounts and store them in an encrypted vault, eliminating the need to remember multiple passwords.

When creating security questions and answers for account recovery, avoid using information that could be easily guessed or found online. Instead, opt for answers that are known only to you and are not publicly available.

Phishing attacks often target individuals to trick them into revealing their passwords or other sensitive information. Be cautious of unsolicited emails, messages, or links that request your login credentials, and verify the legitimacy of such requests before providing any information.

Two-factor authentication (2FA) or multi-factor authentication (MFA) adds an extra layer of security to your accounts by requiring additional verification beyond just a password. Enabling 2FA or MFA wherever possible enhances your account's protection.

Regularly reviewing and updating your passwords is essential, especially for accounts that contain sensitive information or financial data. If you suspect that any of your accounts may have been compromised, change the passwords immediately.

Avoid writing down passwords on physical paper or storing them in easily accessible digital files. If you need to record passwords, consider using a secure and encrypted digital password manager.

Educate yourself and your family or colleagues about the importance of strong and unique passwords. Encourage responsible password practices and promote a culture of cybersecurity awareness.

In summary, crafting strong and unique passwords is a fundamental step in safeguarding your digital accounts and personal information. Strong passwords should be long, complex, and devoid of easily guessable patterns or information. Avoid password reuse, regularly update your passwords, and consider using a reputable password manager for added convenience and security. Additionally, stay vigilant against phishing attempts and embrace two-factor authentication to enhance the protection of your accounts in an increasingly interconnected digital world.

Implementing password management solutions is a crucial step in enhancing cybersecurity and ensuring the secure management of passwords across an organization or individual accounts. Passwords are a fundamental element of digital security, and managing them effectively is essential to protect sensitive data and prevent unauthorized access.

Password management solutions encompass a range of tools and practices designed to simplify the creation, storage, retrieval, and security of passwords. These solutions are particularly valuable in today's digital landscape, where individuals and organizations often have numerous accounts and services, each requiring a unique and strong password.

One common feature of password management solutions is the ability to generate complex and unique passwords for each account. These passwords are typically long, comprising a combination of uppercase and lowercase letters, numbers, and special characters. The use of strong and unique passwords is critical in mitigating the risk of unauthorized access and data breaches.

Password management solutions also offer secure storage for passwords in an encrypted format. Password vaults, a core component of these solutions, protect stored passwords from unauthorized access. This encryption ensures that even if the vault is compromised, the stored passwords remain unreadable to attackers.

One of the primary advantages of password management solutions is the convenience they provide. Users no longer need to remember multiple complex passwords, as the password manager stores and autofills them when needed. This convenience reduces the temptation to use weak passwords or reuse passwords across multiple accounts, improving overall security.

Many password management solutions offer browser extensions and mobile apps, making it easy for users to access their passwords across different devices. This flexibility allows individuals to maintain strong password practices regardless of their location or device.

Additionally, password management solutions often include features such as password sharing and inheritance. These features enable users to securely share passwords with trusted individuals or designate someone to access their passwords in case of an emergency, ensuring access to essential accounts when needed.

Two-factor authentication (2FA) or multi-factor authentication (MFA) is another layer of security often integrated into password management solutions. By requiring an additional verification step beyond the password, 2FA or MFA further enhances the protection of accounts.

Centralized management is a significant benefit for organizations implementing password management solutions. IT administrators can oversee and enforce password policies, monitor user activity, and respond to security incidents more effectively. This centralization streamlines password management across the organization and helps maintain a consistent security posture.

Another critical aspect of password management solutions is their ability to detect and alert users to potential security issues. This includes identifying weak or reused passwords, expiring passwords, or accounts with known security breaches. Such alerts prompt users to take action to strengthen their security posture.

Regularly auditing and rotating passwords is essential for maintaining security. Many password management solutions provide tools to facilitate password rotation and remind users to update their passwords periodically. These practices help protect against unauthorized access, even if a password is compromised.

Password management solutions often include a password generator that can create strong, random passwords according to specified criteria. This eliminates the need for individuals to come up with their passwords, reducing the risk of weak or predictable choices.

User education and training are vital components of implementing password management solutions. Users should be educated on the importance of password security, how to use the password manager effectively, and how to recognize phishing attempts or suspicious login activity.

For organizations, integrating password management solutions into existing security policies and procedures is crucial. This ensures that password management aligns with broader security strategies and compliance requirements.

The choice of a password management solution should align with an organization's specific needs, size, and complexity. There are various commercial and open-source options available, each with its features and capabilities. Evaluating and selecting the right solution is a critical step in the implementation process.

Successful implementation of password management solutions requires careful planning, including assessing existing password practices, selecting an appropriate solution, configuring settings, and training users. It is essential to consider factors such as integration with existing IT infrastructure and compliance requirements.

In summary, implementing password management solutions is a critical step in strengthening cybersecurity and safeguarding sensitive data. These solutions offer the convenience of generating and storing strong and unique passwords, promoting better security practices. Organizations can benefit from centralized management, monitoring, and policy enforcement, while individuals gain a more secure and convenient way to manage their passwords. User education and integration with existing security measures are essential components of a successful implementation. Overall, password management solutions play a vital role in enhancing digital security and reducing the risk of unauthorized access and data breaches in an increasingly interconnected world.

Chapter 4: Safeguarding Your Personal Devices

Device security is a critical aspect of modern digital life, as our devices store and access a wealth of personal and sensitive information. Ensuring the security of these devices is essential to protect our privacy, data, and digital identity.

Device security essentials encompass a range of practices and measures designed to safeguard computers, smartphones, tablets, and other digital devices from various threats, including malware, data breaches, and unauthorized access.

One fundamental aspect of device security is keeping software up to date. Regularly applying operating system and software updates is essential because these updates often contain security patches that address known vulnerabilities. Failing to update software can leave devices exposed to potential attacks.

Installing and maintaining reputable antivirus and anti-malware software is another essential step in device security. These security tools can detect and prevent a wide range of malicious software, including viruses, worms, Trojans, and spyware.

Strong and unique passwords or PINs are crucial for securing access to devices. Passwords should be complex, comprising a combination of letters, numbers, and special characters, and should not be easily guessable. Avoid using common or default passwords.

Two-factor authentication (2FA) or multi-factor authentication (MFA) adds an extra layer of security by requiring an additional verification step beyond the password. Enabling 2FA or MFA wherever possible enhances the protection of device accounts.

Encryption is a powerful tool for securing data on devices. Full-disk encryption ensures that data stored on a device's storage drive is unreadable without the correct decryption key, even if the device falls into the wrong hands.

Regularly backing up data is a crucial practice in device security. Backups ensure that important data can be recovered in the event of device loss, theft, or failure. Cloud-based backup services offer a convenient and secure way to back up data automatically.

Device tracking and remote wipe capabilities are valuable features for smartphones and laptops. These tools enable users to locate lost or stolen devices and remotely erase data to prevent unauthorized access.

Locking devices with a strong passcode, PIN, or biometric authentication (such as fingerprint or facial recognition) is essential to prevent unauthorized physical access. Auto-lock settings should be configured to activate after a short period of inactivity.

Device security also extends to securing Wi-Fi networks. Using strong encryption protocols, changing default router login credentials, and enabling network security features like WPA3 enhance the security of Wi-Fi connections.

Avoiding unsecured public Wi-Fi networks and using a virtual private network (VPN) when connecting to public networks can protect sensitive data from potential eavesdropping or interception.

Regularly reviewing and adjusting privacy settings on devices is essential to control the sharing of personal information with apps and services. Be mindful of the permissions granted to apps and consider whether they are necessary.

Restricting app installations to trusted sources, such as official app stores, reduces the risk of downloading malicious or counterfeit apps. Users should exercise caution when sideloading apps from unverified sources.

Securing email accounts and being cautious of email attachments and links are crucial to prevent phishing attacks and malware distribution. Verify the authenticity of email senders and avoid clicking on suspicious links or downloading unknown attachments.

Implementing device security best practices should extend to all devices, including Internet of Things (IoT) devices, which may have vulnerabilities that can be exploited. Regularly updating and securing IoT devices is essential to prevent potential security breaches.

Regularly reviewing and auditing device security settings and configurations can help identify and address potential vulnerabilities. Users should be proactive in monitoring their device security and responding to any security alerts or notifications.

User education and awareness are vital components of device security. Users should stay informed about the latest threats and security best practices through training and awareness programs. Practicing safe online behavior and exercising caution when interacting with digital content can prevent many security risks.

In summary, device security essentials encompass a range of practices and measures aimed at safeguarding digital devices from various threats. These measures include keeping software up to date, using antivirus and anti-malware software, employing strong passwords and authentication methods, encrypting data, regularly backing up data, and securing Wi-Fi networks. Device security also involves securing email accounts, reviewing privacy settings, and staying informed about the latest threats. By implementing these practices and remaining vigilant, users can significantly enhance the security of their devices and protect their digital lives from potential threats.

Mobile device protection strategies are essential in today's digital landscape, where smartphones and tablets have become integral to our daily lives. These devices store a wealth of personal and sensitive information, making their security a top priority.

One of the fundamental strategies for mobile device protection is implementing strong authentication methods, such as PINs, passwords, biometric recognition (e.g., fingerprint or facial recognition), and two-factor authentication (2FA) or multi-factor authentication (MFA).

Strong authentication adds an extra layer of security to mobile devices, making it significantly more challenging for unauthorized users to gain access to the device and its contents.

Regularly updating the device's operating system and applications is crucial for mobile device protection. Software updates often include security patches that address known vulnerabilities, enhancing the device's resistance to potential threats.

Mobile antivirus and anti-malware applications are valuable tools for detecting and preventing malicious software. These security apps can identify and remove viruses, Trojans, spyware, and other forms of malware that may target mobile devices.

Implementing full-disk encryption on mobile devices is a powerful strategy to protect data from unauthorized access. Encryption ensures that data stored on the device is stored in an unreadable format, making it nearly impossible for attackers to access sensitive information even if they physically possess the device.

Remote tracking and wiping capabilities are essential features for mobile device protection. In the event of loss or theft, these features enable users to track the device's location and remotely erase data to prevent unauthorized access.

Locking the device with a strong passcode, PIN, or biometric authentication is crucial to prevent unauthorized physical access. Enabling auto-lock settings to activate after a short period of inactivity enhances security.

Securing Wi-Fi connections is another critical component of mobile device protection. Avoiding unsecured public Wi-Fi networks and using a virtual private network (VPN) when connecting to public networks can safeguard sensitive data from potential eavesdropping or interception.

Regularly reviewing and adjusting privacy settings on mobile devices is essential to control the sharing of personal information with apps and services. Users should be cautious about granting unnecessary permissions to apps and consider the privacy implications of their choices.

Installing apps only from trusted sources, such as official app stores, reduces the risk of downloading malicious or counterfeit apps. Users should exercise caution when sideloading apps from unverified sources.

Securing email accounts and being cautious of email attachments and links are vital strategies to prevent phishing attacks and malware distribution. Verifying the authenticity of email senders and avoiding clicking on suspicious links or downloading unknown attachments can prevent security risks.

Mobile device protection extends to Internet of Things (IoT) devices, which may have vulnerabilities that can be exploited. Regularly updating and securing IoT devices is essential to prevent potential security breaches.

User education and awareness are crucial aspects of mobile device protection. Users should stay informed about the latest threats and security best practices through training and awareness programs. Practicing safe online behavior and exercising caution when interacting with digital content can prevent many security risks.

In summary, mobile device protection strategies are essential to safeguard smartphones and tablets, which store a wealth of personal and sensitive information. These strategies include strong authentication methods, regular software updates, antivirus and anti-malware applications, full-disk encryption, remote tracking and wiping capabilities, device locking, secure Wi-Fi practices, privacy settings management, app source verification, email security practices, IoT device security, user education, and awareness. By implementing these strategies and remaining vigilant, users can significantly enhance the security of their mobile devices and protect their personal information in an increasingly interconnected digital world.

Chapter 5: Navigating the World of Malware

Identifying different types of malware is essential in understanding the diverse range of malicious software that poses a threat to computer systems, networks, and data. Malware, a contraction of "malicious software," encompasses a wide array of malicious programs and code designed to infiltrate, damage, or gain unauthorized access to computers and digital devices.

One of the most common types of malware is viruses, which are self-replicating programs that attach themselves to legitimate files or programs. Viruses spread when infected files are executed, allowing the virus to replicate and infect other files or systems.

Worms, on the other hand, are standalone malicious programs that do not require a host file to spread. Worms replicate and spread independently by exploiting vulnerabilities in a network or system, making them highly effective at propagating quickly.

Trojans, or Trojan horses, are deceptive malware that masquerade as legitimate software or files to trick users into executing them. Once activated, Trojans can perform a variety of malicious actions, such as stealing data or granting remote access to attackers.

Ransomware is a particularly destructive type of malware that encrypts a victim's files or entire system, rendering them inaccessible. Attackers then demand a ransom payment from the victim in exchange for a decryption key to unlock the files.

Spyware is designed to covertly monitor and collect information about a user's activities, often without their knowledge or consent. This information can include keystrokes, web browsing history, login credentials, and more.

Adware is a form of malware that delivers unwanted advertisements or redirects users to advertising websites.

While adware may not be as harmful as other types of malware, it can be disruptive and negatively impact the user experience.

Rootkits are malware that hide themselves and other malicious programs within a compromised system. Rootkits often have deep access to the operating system, making them challenging to detect and remove.

Keyloggers are a type of spyware that records a user's keystrokes, capturing sensitive information such as usernames, passwords, and credit card details. Attackers can use this data for identity theft or unauthorized access.

Botnets are networks of compromised computers or devices, often controlled by a central command and control server. Botnets can be used for various malicious purposes, such as launching distributed denial of service (DDoS) attacks, sending spam, or conducting large-scale cyberattacks.

Adware is a form of malware that delivers unwanted advertisements or redirects users to advertising websites. While adware may not be as harmful as other types of malware, it can be disruptive and negatively impact the user experience.

Rootkits are malware that hide themselves and other malicious programs within a compromised system. Rootkits often have deep access to the operating system, making them challenging to detect and remove.

Keyloggers are a type of spyware that records a user's keystrokes, capturing sensitive information such as usernames, passwords, and credit card details. Attackers can use this data for identity theft or unauthorized access.

Botnets are networks of compromised computers or devices, often controlled by a central command and control server. Botnets can be used for various malicious purposes, such as launching distributed denial of service (DDoS) attacks, sending spam, or conducting large-scale cyberattacks.

Ransomware is a particularly destructive type of malware that encrypts a victim's files or entire system, rendering them inaccessible. Attackers then demand a ransom payment from the victim in exchange for a decryption key to unlock the files.

Spyware is designed to covertly monitor and collect information about a user's activities, often without their knowledge or consent. This information can include keystrokes, web browsing history, login credentials, and more.

Adware is a form of malware that delivers unwanted advertisements or redirects users to advertising websites. While adware may not be as harmful as other types of malware, it can be disruptive and negatively impact the user experience.

Rootkits are malware that hide themselves and other malicious programs within a compromised system. Rootkits often have deep access to the operating system, making them challenging to detect and remove.

Keyloggers are a type of spyware that records a user's keystrokes, capturing sensitive information such as usernames, passwords, and credit card details. Attackers can use this data for identity theft or unauthorized access.

Botnets are networks of compromised computers or devices, often controlled by a central command and control server. Botnets can be used for various malicious purposes, such as launching distributed denial of service (DDoS) attacks, sending spam, or conducting large-scale cyberattacks.

Fileless malware is a type of malware that operates solely in memory, leaving no traces on a victim's disk storage. This makes it particularly challenging to detect and remove, as traditional antivirus software may struggle to identify it.

Macro malware exploits macros in documents, such as Microsoft Word or Excel files, to deliver malicious code when the document is opened. These macros can execute commands, download additional malware, or perform other malicious actions.

Polymorphic malware is designed to constantly change its code or appearance to evade detection by antivirus programs. Each instance of polymorphic malware appears unique, making it difficult to identify based on known signatures.

Metamorphic malware takes polymorphism a step further by completely rewriting its code each time it infects a new system. This makes it even more challenging for security software to detect and block.

Droppers and downloaders are types of malware that are specifically designed to deliver other malicious payloads to a victim's system. They act as a means of introducing additional malware onto the compromised device.

Malware detection and removal techniques are essential in the ongoing battle against the ever-evolving landscape of malicious software. Detecting and removing malware is critical to maintaining the security and integrity of computer systems, networks, and digital data.

One of the primary techniques for detecting malware is the use of antivirus and anti-malware software. These security tools employ signature-based detection, which involves comparing files and programs against a database of known malware signatures or patterns of malicious code.

Heuristic analysis is another malware detection technique that goes beyond signature-based methods. It involves identifying suspicious behavior or characteristics in programs and files, such as unexpected changes to system settings or unusual network activity.

Behavior-based detection techniques monitor the behavior of programs and processes in real-time to identify deviations from normal behavior. If a program exhibits malicious behavior, such as attempting to modify system files or establish unauthorized network connections, it can be flagged as potential malware.

Anomaly detection relies on establishing a baseline of normal system behavior and then detecting any deviations from that baseline. Unusual or unexpected activities, such as sudden spikes in network traffic or unusual file access patterns, can trigger alerts for further investigation.

Intrusion detection systems (IDS) and intrusion prevention systems (IPS) are security solutions that monitor network traffic for signs of suspicious or malicious activity. They can help identify potential malware infections or attacks in real-time and take action to block or mitigate them.

Sandboxes are isolated environments where suspicious files or programs can be executed safely to observe their behavior. This technique allows security analysts to analyze and assess the actions of potential malware without risking damage to the host system.

Machine learning and artificial intelligence (AI) are increasingly used in malware detection. These technologies can analyze vast amounts of data to identify patterns and anomalies associated with malware, even if the malware has not been previously identified.

Signatureless detection techniques focus on identifying malware without relying on predefined signatures or patterns. They often use advanced algorithms to detect and block previously unknown or zero-day threats.

Network traffic analysis involves monitoring and analyzing network traffic patterns to detect suspicious or malicious activities. This technique can identify malware communications or command-and-control traffic.

Threat intelligence feeds provide up-to-date information about known malware threats and attack vectors. Organizations can use threat intelligence to enhance their malware detection capabilities by proactively identifying and mitigating emerging threats.

Once malware is detected, removal techniques come into play to eliminate the malicious software from infected systems. Common removal techniques include using antivirus or anti-malware software to quarantine or delete the malware.

Manual removal may be necessary for more complex or persistent malware infections. This process involves identifying and manually deleting the malicious files, processes, or registry entries associated with the malware.

System restoration involves restoring the affected system to a known clean state from a backup. This technique ensures that all traces of malware are removed and the system is returned to a secure and operational state.

Reimaging or reinstalling the operating system is a drastic but effective method for removing malware. It involves completely erasing the infected system's hard drive and reinstalling the operating system and software from scratch.

Security patches and updates should be applied to address vulnerabilities that may have been exploited by the malware. Keeping software and systems up to date is essential to prevent future infections.

Isolation of infected systems from the network can prevent the spread of malware to other devices. Isolated systems can be cleaned and restored without risking further contamination.

Data recovery and backup restoration are critical after malware removal to ensure that any lost or encrypted data is recovered and restored to its original state. Regular backups are essential for minimizing data loss in the event of a malware infection.

Educating users and employees about safe computing practices and recognizing phishing attempts can help prevent malware infections from occurring in the first place. User awareness is a crucial component of a robust defense against malware.

Continuous monitoring and threat hunting are essential to identify and respond to emerging threats and potential reinfections. Proactive monitoring and rapid incident response can minimize the impact of malware infections.

Collaboration with cybersecurity experts, incident response teams, and law enforcement agencies may be necessary in the case of advanced or targeted malware attacks. These experts can provide specialized expertise and resources for malware removal and investigation.

In summary, malware detection and removal techniques are essential in combating the diverse and evolving landscape of malicious software. Detection methods range from signature-based and heuristic analysis to behavior-based and anomaly detection techniques. Removal techniques include antivirus software, manual removal, system restoration, reimaging, security patching, isolation, data recovery, and user education. Effective malware detection and removal require a combination of these techniques and a proactive approach to cybersecurity to protect against current and emerging threats.

Chapter 6: Cyberwatch Tools and Techniques

An overview of Cyberwatch tools provides insight into the diverse set of resources and technologies available for enhancing cybersecurity practices and defending against cyber threats in an increasingly digital world. These tools encompass a wide range of capabilities, from threat detection and analysis to vulnerability assessment and incident response.

One fundamental category of Cyberwatch tools focuses on threat detection and monitoring. These tools continuously analyze network traffic, system logs, and endpoint activities to identify suspicious or malicious behavior indicative of cyber threats.

Intrusion detection systems (IDS) are one such tool, capable of recognizing unauthorized access attempts, anomalous patterns, and known attack signatures. Intrusion prevention systems (IPS) can take immediate action to block or mitigate detected threats.

Security information and event management (SIEM) solutions aggregate and correlate data from various sources to provide a holistic view of an organization's security posture. SIEM tools enable security analysts to detect and respond to security incidents effectively.

Endpoint detection and response (EDR) solutions focus on monitoring and securing individual devices, such as laptops and smartphones. EDR tools provide real-time visibility into endpoint activities, allowing for rapid threat detection and incident response.

Network traffic analysis tools monitor and analyze data flows within a network to detect anomalies, malicious activities, or potential breaches. These tools can help organizations identify and respond to threats in real-time.

Threat intelligence platforms provide organizations with up-to-date information about emerging threats, vulnerabilities, and attack tactics. This data empowers cybersecurity teams to proactively defend against known and emerging threats.

Vulnerability assessment tools play a crucial role in identifying weaknesses and potential entry points for attackers. These tools scan systems, applications, and networks for known vulnerabilities, helping organizations prioritize and remediate security issues.

Penetration testing tools, also known as ethical hacking tools, simulate cyberattacks to assess an organization's security defenses. Penetration testers use these tools to identify vulnerabilities and weaknesses before malicious actors can exploit them.

Cybersecurity orchestration and automation platforms streamline incident response processes by automating routine tasks and facilitating collaboration among security teams. These tools enable organizations to respond more efficiently to security incidents.

Firewalls and intrusion prevention systems (IPS) are essential network security tools that filter incoming and outgoing traffic, blocking potentially malicious data and ensuring network security.

Endpoint protection platforms (EPP) combine antivirus, anti-malware, and other security features to safeguard individual devices from a wide range of threats, including viruses, ransomware, and spyware.

Email security solutions use advanced filtering and threat detection techniques to protect against phishing emails, malware attachments, and other email-based threats.

Secure web gateways (SWG) filter web traffic, blocking access to malicious websites and preventing users from inadvertently downloading malware or accessing malicious content.

Data loss prevention (DLP) tools monitor and protect sensitive data by preventing unauthorized access, sharing, or leakage of confidential information.

Security awareness training platforms educate employees about cybersecurity best practices, ensuring that they can recognize and respond to potential threats and phishing attempts.

Security incident and event management (SIEM) systems provide real-time monitoring, analysis, and reporting of security events, helping organizations detect and respond to security incidents promptly.

Security information sharing and analysis centers (ISACs) and threat intelligence sharing platforms enable organizations to share and receive information about emerging threats and attack tactics, enhancing collective cybersecurity defense.

Security assessment and compliance tools help organizations assess their security posture, ensure compliance with industry regulations, and identify areas requiring improvement.

Security orchestration, automation, and response (SOAR) platforms integrate cybersecurity tools and processes, enabling automated incident response and efficient threat mitigation.

Security analytics and machine learning solutions leverage artificial intelligence and advanced analytics to detect and respond to threats more effectively, even in complex and rapidly evolving threat landscapes.

Security testing tools, such as vulnerability scanners and penetration testing software, evaluate the security of systems, applications, and networks to identify and remediate vulnerabilities.

Identity and access management (IAM) solutions manage user access and authentication, ensuring that only authorized individuals can access specific resources and data.

Security incident response platforms (SIRPs) centralize incident response processes, providing a unified interface for managing and coordinating security incidents and investigations.

Endpoint detection and response (EDR) solutions offer real-time monitoring, threat detection, and incident response capabilities specifically focused on individual devices and endpoints.

Security assessment and risk management tools assist organizations in identifying and prioritizing security risks, enabling informed decision-making to mitigate potential threats.

Security awareness and training platforms deliver cybersecurity education and awareness programs to employees, enhancing their ability to recognize and respond to security threats.

Patch management solutions automate the process of applying software updates and patches to eliminate known vulnerabilities and enhance overall system security.

Threat hunting tools empower cybersecurity teams to proactively search for signs of potential threats and anomalies within their network environments, enabling early threat detection and mitigation.

Intrusion prevention systems (IPS) go beyond intrusion detection by actively blocking and preventing unauthorized access attempts, enhancing network security.

Next-generation firewalls (NGFWs) combine traditional firewall capabilities with advanced features like application-layer filtering and threat intelligence, providing comprehensive network protection.

In summary, the landscape of Cyberwatch tools is vast and diverse, encompassing a wide array of solutions designed to bolster cybersecurity efforts. From threat detection and monitoring tools to vulnerability assessment and risk management solutions, these tools play a pivotal role in defending against cyber threats and safeguarding digital assets in an interconnected world. Organizations must carefully evaluate their unique security needs and objectives to select and deploy the most effective Cyberwatch tools to enhance their cybersecurity posture and protect against evolving threats.

Advanced Cyberwatch strategies are essential for organizations seeking to stay ahead of evolving cyber threats and protect their digital assets effectively. These strategies build upon foundational cybersecurity measures to address sophisticated and persistent threats in an increasingly complex and interconnected digital landscape.

One crucial aspect of advanced Cyberwatch strategies is threat intelligence integration. Organizations leverage threat intelligence feeds and services to gain insights into emerging threats, vulnerabilities, and attacker tactics. This intelligence enables proactive threat detection and informs cybersecurity decision-making.

Continuous monitoring and real-time threat detection are fundamental components of advanced strategies. Organizations implement Security Information and Event Management (SIEM) solutions to collect and analyze vast amounts of data from various sources, helping identify anomalies and potential security incidents promptly.

Automation plays a significant role in advanced Cyberwatch strategies. Security orchestration and automation platforms enable organizations to automate routine security tasks, streamline incident response processes, and reduce the manual workload on cybersecurity teams.

Advanced analytics and machine learning are critical for identifying complex threats. These technologies analyze patterns and anomalies in data to detect sophisticated attack techniques that may evade traditional security measures.

Threat hunting is a proactive approach used in advanced Cyberwatch strategies. Cybersecurity professionals actively search for signs of potential threats within their network environments, using specialized tools and expertise to uncover hidden threats.

Zero-trust security models are gaining prominence in advanced strategies. They assume that no entity, whether inside or outside the organization, should be trusted by default. Zero-trust architectures require rigorous identity verification, continuous monitoring, and strict access controls.

Endpoint detection and response (EDR) solutions are a key element in advanced strategies. EDR tools provide real-time visibility into endpoint activities, allowing for rapid threat detection, investigation, and response.

Cloud security strategies are essential as organizations increasingly migrate to cloud environments. Advanced Cyberwatch strategies include cloud-native security solutions that protect data and workloads in cloud platforms, ensuring a comprehensive security posture.

Security automation and orchestration are integral components of advanced strategies. Automated workflows and responses enable organizations to respond swiftly to security incidents, reducing the time attackers have to carry out malicious activities.

Advanced Cyberwatch strategies prioritize threat intelligence sharing and collaboration. Organizations participate in Information Sharing and Analysis Centers (ISACs) and share threat information with peers to enhance collective cybersecurity defense.

Multi-factor authentication (MFA) or two-factor authentication (2FA) is a standard practice in advanced strategies. These authentication methods add an extra layer of security by requiring users to provide multiple forms of verification, reducing the risk of unauthorized access.

Security awareness and training programs are continuously updated in advanced strategies to educate employees about evolving threats and security best practices. Regular training helps employees recognize and respond to potential security risks effectively.

Advanced strategies emphasize security culture and governance within organizations. Senior leadership fosters a culture of security awareness, making cybersecurity a priority throughout the organization.

Red teaming and penetration testing are employed to assess an organization's security posture rigorously. These techniques simulate real-world cyberattacks to identify vulnerabilities and weaknesses that may not be apparent through traditional assessments.

Incident response plans and tabletop exercises are regularly practiced in advanced strategies to ensure organizations are well-prepared to respond to security incidents effectively. These exercises help validate the effectiveness of incident response procedures.

Threat intelligence fusion centers consolidate and analyze threat data from various sources, enhancing an organization's ability to detect and respond to advanced threats. These centers provide a centralized hub for threat intelligence analysis and dissemination.

Security data lakes and advanced analytics platforms enable organizations to collect, store, and analyze vast amounts of security data for threat detection and investigation. These platforms help identify patterns and trends that may indicate emerging threats.

Advanced Cyberwatch strategies incorporate the use of deception technologies, such as honeypots and deception networks, to lure attackers away from critical systems and gather valuable threat intelligence.

Cybersecurity operations centers (SOCs) are at the heart of advanced strategies, providing 24/7 monitoring, incident response, and threat analysis capabilities. SOCs leverage advanced tools and expertise to defend against sophisticated threats.

Continuous red teaming and adversary simulation exercises challenge an organization's defenses and help identify weaknesses that may not be evident through standard security assessments.

Advanced Cyberwatch strategies also involve collaboration with law enforcement agencies, incident response teams, and threat-sharing communities to respond to and investigate cyberattacks effectively.

Advanced strategies prioritize proactive threat hunting to identify and eliminate threats before they can cause damage or exfiltrate data.

In summary, advanced Cyberwatch strategies are essential for organizations to stay ahead of sophisticated and evolving cyber threats. These strategies leverage threat intelligence, automation, advanced analytics, threat hunting, and a culture of security to proactively detect, respond to, and mitigate cyber risks. By implementing advanced Cyberwatch strategies, organizations can enhance their cybersecurity posture and effectively protect their digital assets in an ever-changing threat landscape.

Chapter 7: Securing Your Online Identity

Managing and protecting online identities is of paramount importance in today's digital age, where individuals and organizations interact and transact online extensively. An online identity encompasses the digital footprint, persona, and reputation one establishes through their online activities, and safeguarding it is crucial for privacy and security.

Individuals must begin by understanding that their online identity extends beyond social media profiles, encompassing email accounts, online shopping accounts, and even comments posted on websites and forums.

The first step in managing and protecting one's online identity is creating strong and unique passwords for each online account, as using the same password across multiple accounts increases vulnerability to hacking and identity theft.

Password management tools can assist in generating and securely storing complex passwords, simplifying the process of safeguarding online accounts.

Two-factor authentication (2FA) or multi-factor authentication (MFA) should be enabled whenever possible, as it adds an extra layer of security by requiring a second form of verification, such as a code sent to a mobile device or biometric data.

Regularly reviewing privacy settings on social media platforms is essential, as these settings dictate who can access and view personal information, posts, and photos.

Individuals should be cautious about the information they share online, avoiding the disclosure of sensitive personal details, such as home addresses, phone numbers, and financial information.

When creating usernames or handles for online platforms, it is advisable to avoid using real names or easily identifiable information to protect one's anonymity.

Managing the content one shares online is crucial, as anything posted on the internet can potentially be accessed and used by others, even if deleted.

Being cautious about accepting friend or connection requests from unknown individuals can help reduce the risk of connecting with malicious actors who may attempt to exploit personal information.

Online reputation management involves monitoring search engine results and social media mentions to ensure that the information associated with one's name or brand remains positive and accurate.

Search engine optimization (SEO) techniques can be employed to promote positive content and suppress negative or undesirable search results.

Regularly reviewing online accounts and permissions granted to third-party applications can help individuals maintain control over their digital presence and limit the access others have to their data. Phishing attacks are common methods used by cybercriminals to steal personal information, and individuals should be vigilant in recognizing phishing emails and messages, avoiding clicking on suspicious links or downloading attachments from unknown sources. Cybersecurity awareness and education are critical for understanding the evolving tactics used by cybercriminals to compromise online identities and staying informed about emerging threats. Businesses and organizations must also prioritize managing and protecting their online identities, as reputational damage can have significant financial and operational consequences.

Implementing robust cybersecurity measures, such as firewalls, intrusion detection systems, and antivirus software, can help protect online assets and sensitive customer information.

Employee training and awareness programs are essential for ensuring that staff members understand the importance of cybersecurity and are vigilant against social engineering attacks.

Online brand monitoring tools can assist organizations in tracking mentions and conversations related to their brand, allowing them to address customer concerns and protect their reputation.

Businesses should have incident response plans in place to effectively manage and mitigate the impact of cybersecurity incidents on their online identity.

Regularly monitoring and analyzing website traffic and user behavior can help organizations detect and respond to suspicious activities, such as fraudulent account creation or unauthorized access attempts.

Encryption and secure communication protocols should be used to protect sensitive customer data, ensuring that it remains confidential and secure during transmission.

In summary, managing and protecting online identities is a shared responsibility for individuals and organizations in an increasingly interconnected digital world. Individuals must take steps to safeguard their personal information and practice cybersecurity best practices, while businesses and organizations must implement robust security measures and prioritize customer data protection. By proactively managing and protecting online identities, both individuals and organizations can reduce the risk of identity theft, reputational damage, and cybersecurity incidents, ensuring a safer and more secure online experience for all. Safeguarding personal information on the web is a critical concern in today's digital age, where individuals routinely share sensitive data online.

The internet has revolutionized how we live, work, and communicate, but it has also exposed our personal information to various risks, including identity theft, data breaches, and online scams.

Whether we are shopping online, using social media, or managing our finances through web-based platforms, our personal information is constantly at risk of being compromised.

The first step in safeguarding personal information on the web is to understand what constitutes sensitive data.

Sensitive information includes personal identifiers, such as Social Security numbers, passport numbers, and driver's license numbers, which can be used for identity theft.

Financial information, including credit card numbers, bank account details, and payment card information, is highly valuable to cybercriminals seeking to steal money or commit fraud. Medical records and healthcare data are also sensitive, as they contain private information about an individual's health conditions, treatments, and prescriptions.

Personal contact information, such as email addresses, phone numbers, and physical addresses, can be exploited by spammers, scammers, or cyberstalkers.

Online login credentials, including usernames and passwords, are prime targets for cybercriminals seeking unauthorized access to accounts and sensitive information.

To safeguard personal information, individuals must adopt a proactive approach to online privacy and security.

Using strong and unique passwords for each online account is fundamental, as weak or reused passwords can lead to unauthorized access.

Password managers are valuable tools for generating, storing, and managing complex passwords, reducing the risk of password-related breaches.

Enabling two-factor authentication (2FA) whenever possible provides an additional layer of security by requiring a second form of verification, such as a code sent to a mobile device or biometric data.

Regularly reviewing and updating privacy settings on social media platforms and online accounts ensures that personal information is only shared with trusted individuals.

Being cautious about sharing personal information on social media, including birthdates, addresses, and family details, can help protect against identity theft and scams.

Phishing attacks, where cybercriminals impersonate legitimate entities to trick individuals into revealing personal information, are common online threats.

Recognizing phishing emails and messages is crucial, and individuals should avoid clicking on suspicious links or downloading attachments from unknown sources.

Keeping software, operating systems, and antivirus programs up to date is essential, as updates often include security patches to protect against known vulnerabilities.

Secure web browsing practices, such as avoiding unsecured websites and using virtual private networks (VPNs) on public Wi-Fi networks, can safeguard personal information from interception and data theft.

Regularly monitoring financial statements and accounts for unauthorized or suspicious activity is vital for early detection of identity theft or fraud.

When disposing of old computers or mobile devices, individuals should ensure that all personal data is securely wiped from the device's storage.

Regularly checking one's credit report for unusual or unauthorized activity is recommended to detect signs of identity theft.

Online shopping and financial transactions should only be conducted on secure websites that display a padlock symbol and use HTTPS encryption.

Securing personal devices with strong passwords or biometric authentication and enabling device encryption can protect sensitive data in case of theft or loss.

Using antivirus and anti-malware software helps detect and remove malicious software that may compromise personal information.

Protecting personal information is not limited to individuals alone; organizations and businesses also have a responsibility to safeguard customer data and maintain trust.

Data encryption should be employed to secure customer information during storage and transmission, ensuring that it remains confidential and protected from unauthorized access.

Implementing robust cybersecurity measures, such as firewalls, intrusion detection systems, and intrusion prevention systems, can protect against data breaches and cyberattacks.

Employee training and awareness programs are essential for ensuring that staff members understand their role in protecting customer data and recognize potential security threats.

Data breach response plans should be in place to manage and mitigate the impact of security incidents on customer information.

Regularly reviewing and updating privacy policies and terms of service helps organizations maintain transparency and compliance with data protection regulations.

Engaging in responsible data handling practices, such as collecting only necessary customer information and securely disposing of outdated data, promotes trust and privacy.

Collaborating with cybersecurity experts and threat intelligence sources can enhance an organization's ability to detect and respond to evolving threats and vulnerabilities.

In summary, safeguarding personal information on the web is a shared responsibility between individuals and organizations in an increasingly digital world. Individuals must adopt proactive online privacy and security practices, including using strong passwords, enabling 2FA, and recognizing phishing attempts. Organizations, on the other hand, must implement robust cybersecurity measures, educate employees, and prioritize data protection to maintain trust and safeguard customer information. By working together, individuals and organizations can navigate the digital landscape while preserving privacy and security.

Chapter 8: Protecting Your Data in the Cloud

Cloud security considerations are of utmost importance as organizations increasingly rely on cloud computing services to store, process, and manage their data and applications.

Cloud computing offers numerous benefits, including scalability, flexibility, and cost-efficiency, but it also introduces new security challenges and risks that must be carefully managed.

One fundamental consideration in cloud security is data protection, as organizations must ensure the confidentiality, integrity, and availability of their data stored in the cloud.

Encryption is a crucial tool for securing data in transit and at rest, and organizations should encrypt sensitive data both before it leaves their premises and while it is stored in the cloud.

Access control and identity management are critical aspects of cloud security, as organizations need to manage who can access their cloud resources and ensure that only authorized users can interact with sensitive data.

Implementing strong authentication methods, such as multi-factor authentication (MFA), helps prevent unauthorized access to cloud accounts and services.

Regularly reviewing and auditing user access permissions to cloud resources helps ensure that individuals have the appropriate level of access based on their roles and responsibilities within the organization.

Another significant consideration in cloud security is network security, as organizations need to protect the communication channels between their on-premises infrastructure and cloud services.

Firewalls, intrusion detection systems, and virtual private networks (VPNs) can help secure network connections and prevent unauthorized access to cloud resources.

Secure cloud configurations are essential, and organizations should follow best practices and guidelines provided by cloud service providers to configure their cloud resources securely.

Patch management is critical in maintaining the security of cloud-based systems, as vulnerabilities in cloud services or applications can be exploited by attackers.

Data backup and disaster recovery planning should be part of cloud security strategies to ensure data can be recovered in case of data loss or service disruptions.

Security monitoring and incident response capabilities are essential in detecting and responding to security threats and incidents in the cloud.

Organizations should continuously monitor cloud resources for suspicious activities, configure alerts for security events, and have incident response plans in place.

Cloud service providers often offer security tools and services, such as security information and event management (SIEM) solutions and threat detection services, which can enhance cloud security.

It is essential for organizations to understand their responsibilities in a shared responsibility model, where the cloud service provider is responsible for the security of the cloud infrastructure, while the customer is responsible for securing their data and applications.

Compliance with regulatory requirements and industry standards is another critical consideration, as organizations must ensure that their cloud deployments adhere to data protection and privacy regulations.

Regularly assessing and auditing cloud security controls can help organizations maintain compliance and demonstrate due diligence in protecting customer data.

Employee training and awareness programs play a vital role in cloud security, as employees need to understand security best practices, the risks associated with cloud computing, and how to recognize and report security threats.

Secure development practices should be employed when developing and deploying cloud-based applications to minimize security vulnerabilities and risks.

Third-party risk management is essential, as organizations need to evaluate the security practices of cloud service providers and third-party vendors who have access to their cloud resources.

Creating incident response plans specifically tailored to cloud environments ensures that organizations can respond effectively to security incidents and minimize their impact.

Cloud security considerations also include data sovereignty and residency, as organizations need to understand where their data is stored and ensure compliance with data protection regulations in different regions.

Regularly testing and assessing cloud security controls through vulnerability assessments and penetration testing helps identify weaknesses and vulnerabilities that could be exploited by attackers.

Collaboration and information sharing within the cloud security community can provide valuable insights and threat intelligence to help organizations stay informed about emerging threats.

In summary, cloud security considerations encompass a wide range of factors that organizations must address to protect their data and applications in the cloud.

Data protection, access control, network security, secure configurations, patch management, and incident response are all essential elements of a robust cloud security strategy.

Compliance with regulations, employee training, secure development practices, and third-party risk management are also critical components.

By carefully addressing these considerations and staying vigilant in monitoring and responding to security threats, organizations can leverage the benefits of cloud computing while maintaining the security and integrity of their data and systems.

Data backup and recovery in cloud environments is a critical aspect of ensuring the availability, integrity, and security of digital assets.

Organizations entrust cloud service providers with their data, applications, and infrastructure, making it essential to have robust backup and recovery strategies in place.

Data loss can occur due to various factors, including hardware failures, software errors, human errors, malicious attacks, and natural disasters.

To mitigate the risk of data loss, organizations must regularly back up their data stored in the cloud to secure and resilient storage solutions.

Cloud providers often offer backup and disaster recovery services that enable organizations to create copies of their data and systems, ensuring they can be quickly restored in case of data loss or service disruptions.

These backup services typically offer automated and scheduled backups, ensuring that data is consistently and reliably backed up.

Backup retention policies determine how long backup copies are retained, allowing organizations to align their data recovery strategies with their specific needs and compliance requirements.

In addition to data backup, organizations must also consider the recovery aspect of their cloud data management strategies.

Data recovery encompasses the process of retrieving and restoring data from backups to its original or alternative location, ensuring minimal downtime and disruption to business operations.

A critical consideration in data recovery is the Recovery Time Objective (RTO), which specifies the maximum acceptable downtime for a system or application.

Organizations must determine their RTO based on their business needs and priorities, as it influences the selection of backup and recovery solutions.

Another important metric is the Recovery Point Objective (RPO), which defines the maximum acceptable data loss in case of a failure.

Cloud-based backup and recovery solutions should align with the organization's RPO and RTO goals to meet recovery expectations effectively.

Cloud providers often offer high availability and disaster recovery solutions that enable organizations to fail over to alternative environments in case of an outage, minimizing service disruption.

Testing and regular drills of disaster recovery plans and procedures are essential to ensure that data recovery processes work as expected and within the defined RTO and RPO parameters.

Backup and recovery in the cloud should encompass a wide range of data types, including files, databases, configurations, virtual machines, and application data.

Data should be protected with encryption both in transit and at rest during the backup and recovery process to maintain data security and compliance.

Organizations should also implement access controls and authentication mechanisms to ensure that only authorized personnel can perform data recovery operations.

Monitoring and alerting systems should be in place to provide visibility into the backup and recovery processes and to detect any anomalies or issues that may require immediate attention.

Data backup and recovery strategies should consider data versioning, allowing organizations to recover data from different points in time, which can be crucial for addressing data corruption or accidental deletion.

Cross-region or cross-cloud backups are valuable for redundancy and disaster recovery, ensuring that data remains accessible even in the event of regional outages or provider-specific issues.

Data recovery testing should include validating the integrity of backed-up data and verifying that the restored data is usable and consistent with the organization's requirements.

A comprehensive documentation of backup and recovery procedures, including step-by-step instructions, contact information for support, and escalation paths, is essential for efficient and effective data recovery.

Organizations should also establish communication protocols for notifying relevant stakeholders in the event of a data loss incident or disaster recovery activation.

Regularly reviewing and updating backup and recovery plans ensures that they remain aligned with changing business needs, technological advancements, and evolving threats.

Compliance with data protection and privacy regulations, such as GDPR or HIPAA, is a critical consideration in data backup and recovery, as organizations must ensure that data is handled in accordance with legal requirements.

Cloud service providers often offer data governance and compliance tools that can assist organizations in meeting their regulatory obligations.

The cost of data backup and recovery in the cloud should be carefully considered, as it can vary based on factors such as the volume of data, storage solutions selected, and the frequency of backups.

Organizations should weigh the costs against the potential financial and reputational losses associated with data loss and downtime.

In summary, data backup and recovery in cloud environments are essential for safeguarding digital assets, ensuring data availability, and mitigating the impact of data loss incidents.

Organizations must carefully plan, implement, and test their backup and recovery strategies to align with their business needs, recovery objectives, and compliance requirements.

By adopting a proactive and comprehensive approach to data backup and recovery in the cloud, organizations can maintain business continuity and protect their valuable data assets.

Chapter 9: Social Engineering Awareness

Understanding social engineering tactics is crucial in today's interconnected digital world, as cybercriminals increasingly rely on human manipulation to achieve their malicious objectives.

Social engineering is a form of psychological manipulation that exploits human behaviors, trust, and cognitive biases to trick individuals into divulging confidential information, performing certain actions, or compromising their security.

One common social engineering tactic is phishing, where attackers use fraudulent emails, messages, or websites that appear legitimate to deceive recipients into revealing sensitive information, such as login credentials or financial details.

Phishing emails often mimic trusted organizations or individuals and use urgency or fear to prompt quick responses.

Another social engineering technique is pretexting, where an attacker fabricates a plausible scenario or pretext to extract information from a target.

Pretexting often involves building a false sense of trust and credibility through detailed impersonation.

Baiting is a social engineering tactic where attackers offer something enticing, such as free software or downloads, to lure victims into clicking on malicious links or downloading malware.

Vishing, or voice phishing, involves phone calls where attackers impersonate trusted entities, such as tech support, government agencies, or financial institutions, to trick victims into disclosing sensitive information or performing actions.

Quid pro quo is a tactic where attackers offer something valuable in exchange for information, such as promising IT support or free software in return for access credentials.

Tailgating or piggybacking occurs when an attacker gains physical access to a restricted area by following an authorized person without raising suspicion.

Impersonation involves attackers posing as trusted individuals or authorities, such as colleagues, executives, or law enforcement officers, to manipulate victims into complying with their requests.

Social engineers often use reverse social engineering, where they manipulate victims into approaching them for help or assistance, making the victim feel vulnerable and more likely to cooperate.

Online manipulation techniques, such as catfishing, involve creating fake online personas to establish relationships, gain trust, and extract information or money from victims.

Fear and intimidation tactics may be used by social engineers to pressure victims into disclosing information or complying with their demands.

Social engineers leverage the principle of authority, convincing victims that they are figures of authority or experts to gain compliance.

Reciprocity is another psychological principle used in social engineering, where attackers provide small favors or compliments to create a sense of obligation in victims.

Scarcity tactics, such as claiming limited availability or urgency, push victims to take quick actions without thinking critically.

Understanding the psychology behind social engineering tactics is essential for individuals and organizations to recognize and defend against these manipulative techniques.

Raising awareness and educating employees about social engineering threats is a critical step in preventing successful attacks.

Training programs should teach individuals to verify requests for sensitive information or actions, especially when they come from unfamiliar or unexpected sources.

Organizations should implement security policies and procedures that include authentication protocols for verifying the identity of individuals requesting access or information.

Implementing multi-factor authentication (MFA) can add an extra layer of security, making it harder for attackers to gain unauthorized access.

Employees should be encouraged to report suspicious requests or incidents promptly to the organization's security team.

Creating a culture of security awareness within an organization can help employees recognize and respond to social engineering attempts effectively.

Regular security awareness training should cover a variety of social engineering tactics, real-life examples, and practical guidance for identifying and mitigating threats.

Implementing robust cybersecurity measures, such as email filtering, intrusion detection systems, and endpoint protection, can help detect and prevent social engineering attacks.

Organizations should regularly assess and test their security controls to identify vulnerabilities and weaknesses that could be exploited by social engineers.

Security policies and procedures should be continually updated to address emerging social engineering threats and tactics.

Collaboration with law enforcement and cybersecurity experts can aid in investigating and mitigating social engineering attacks, as well as identifying and apprehending perpetrators.

Individuals and organizations should remain vigilant and cautious when receiving unsolicited requests for information or actions, especially when they involve sensitive data or financial transactions.

In summary, understanding social engineering tactics is vital for individuals and organizations to defend against this prevalent and evolving threat.

By recognizing the various psychological manipulation techniques used by social engineers, individuals can become more resilient to these attacks and protect their personal information and organizational assets.

Educating employees, implementing security measures, and fostering a culture of security awareness are essential steps in mitigating the risks posed by social engineering tactics and ensuring a safer digital environment.

Detecting and preventing social engineering attacks is a critical component of modern cybersecurity strategies, as these attacks rely on psychological manipulation to exploit human vulnerabilities.

Social engineering attacks come in various forms, including phishing, pretexting, baiting, vishing, impersonation, and more.

Phishing attacks, for example, involve deceptive emails or messages that appear legitimate to trick recipients into revealing sensitive information or clicking on malicious links.

Pretexting relies on fabricated scenarios or pretexts to manipulate individuals into divulging personal or confidential information.

Baiting lures victims with enticing offers, such as free downloads or prizes, to entice them into engaging in risky actions.

Vishing attacks use phone calls to impersonate trusted entities and extract sensitive data or actions from victims.

Impersonation tactics involve attackers posing as authority figures or trusted individuals to manipulate victims.

Detecting social engineering attacks often requires a combination of technical solutions and human vigilance.

Email filtering systems can help identify and block phishing emails by analyzing content and identifying suspicious links or attachments.

Antivirus and anti-malware software can detect and prevent malware delivered through social engineering attacks.

Educating employees about social engineering tactics and red flags is crucial, as they are often the first line of defense.

Employees should be trained to recognize phishing emails, verify the authenticity of requests, and report suspicious incidents promptly.

Establishing clear protocols for verifying requests for sensitive information or actions can help prevent successful social engineering attacks.

Implementing multi-factor authentication (MFA) can add an additional layer of security by requiring multiple forms of verification.

Organizations should regularly update their security policies and procedures to address emerging social engineering threats and tactics.

Monitoring network traffic and user behavior can help identify unusual or suspicious activities indicative of social engineering attacks.

Creating a culture of security awareness within an organization fosters a sense of responsibility and vigilance among employees.

Regular security awareness training should cover a wide range of social engineering tactics, real-life examples, and practical guidance.

Employees should be encouraged to report any incidents or suspicious requests to the organization's security team.

Implementing intrusion detection systems (IDS) and intrusion prevention systems (IPS) can help detect and block social engineering attacks in real-time.

Security incident response plans should be in place to handle and mitigate the impact of social engineering incidents.

Collaborating with law enforcement and cybersecurity experts can aid in investigating and prosecuting social engineering perpetrators.

Fostering a strong relationship between the organization's security team and employees can lead to more effective incident reporting and response.

Incorporating psychological principles into security awareness training can help individuals understand the tactics and motivations behind social engineering attacks.

Simulated social engineering tests, such as phishing exercises, can help organizations assess their vulnerability to these attacks and improve their defenses.

Creating a robust cybersecurity policy that includes guidelines for social engineering prevention and response is essential.

Security policies should address data protection, access controls, and incident handling procedures related to social engineering attacks.

Regularly testing and auditing security controls, such as access permissions and authentication methods, can identify vulnerabilities exploited in social engineering attacks.

Implementing advanced authentication solutions, such as biometrics or behavioral analysis, can enhance security against social engineering threats.

Organizations should engage in threat intelligence sharing and collaboration to stay informed about emerging social engineering tactics and trends.

In summary, detecting and preventing social engineering attacks require a multi-pronged approach that combines technical solutions, employee education, and robust security policies.

By understanding the psychology behind these attacks and fostering a culture of security awareness, organizations can enhance their defenses against social engineering threats.

Regular testing, monitoring, and collaboration with cybersecurity experts are essential to stay one step ahead of evolving social engineering tactics and protect sensitive data and assets.

Chapter 10: Developing a Cybersecurity Mindset

The psychology of cybersecurity delves into the intricate interplay between human behavior, cognition, and digital security measures.

Understanding how individuals perceive and interact with cybersecurity plays a pivotal role in developing effective defense strategies against cyber threats.

Human beings, by nature, are susceptible to cognitive biases and vulnerabilities that can be exploited by cybercriminals.

One of the fundamental psychological aspects of cybersecurity is the concept of risk perception.

People tend to underestimate certain risks, such as falling victim to cyberattacks, especially when those risks appear abstract or remote.

Cybersecurity professionals must bridge this perception gap by effectively communicating the potential consequences of security breaches and the importance of preventive measures.

The phenomenon of optimism bias often leads individuals to believe that they are less likely to experience negative events than others.

This bias can result in individuals taking fewer precautions when it comes to cybersecurity, assuming that they are immune to cyber threats.

The psychology of passwords reveals that many individuals favor convenience over security.

People often choose easily memorable passwords, reuse them across multiple accounts, and fail to update them regularly, making their accounts vulnerable to breaches.

Behavioral economics plays a significant role in understanding cybersecurity decisions, as individuals tend to favor immediate gratification over long-term security.

This can lead to impulsive clicking on suspicious links, downloading unverified files, or ignoring security warnings.

The fear of missing out (FOMO) can also drive individuals to take risks online, such as clicking on enticing offers or participating in unverified online activities.

Social proof, another psychological principle, influences individuals to follow the crowd, even when it comes to cybersecurity decisions.

If people see others engaging in risky online behavior, they may be more likely to mimic those actions.

Cybersecurity fatigue is a phenomenon where individuals become overwhelmed by the constant need for security-related decisions and actions.

As a result, they may become complacent or apathetic toward security measures, potentially leaving them vulnerable to cyberattacks.

Understanding the psychology of phishing attacks is critical, as phishing is one of the most prevalent and successful cyber threats.

Phishers exploit human emotions, such as fear, curiosity, or urgency, to manipulate individuals into revealing sensitive information.

Phishing emails often create a sense of urgency, leading recipients to act hastily without considering the risks.

The psychology of social engineering attacks, such as pretexting or impersonation, involves building trust and credibility.

Attackers craft convincing personas or scenarios to manipulate victims into divulging information or performing actions that compromise security.

Cognitive biases, such as confirmation bias, can lead individuals to seek information that aligns with their preexisting beliefs, making them susceptible to misinformation or disinformation campaigns.

Understanding the psychology of cybersecurity awareness is essential for designing effective training programs.

Training should focus on changing behaviors, not just increasing knowledge, by addressing cognitive biases and encouraging proactive security measures.

The mere exposure effect, a psychological phenomenon, suggests that individuals tend to develop a preference for things they are exposed to repeatedly.

Cybersecurity messages and best practices should be consistently reinforced to create lasting behavioral change.

Fear appeals, while effective in some cases, can backfire if they create overwhelming anxiety or a sense of helplessness.

Effective cybersecurity education balances the presentation of threats with actionable steps individuals can take to protect themselves.

The psychology of cybersecurity decision-making extends to organizations as well.

Institutional factors, such as organizational culture and leadership, influence the prioritization of cybersecurity within a company.

Organizations with a strong cybersecurity culture are more likely to promote secure behaviors among employees.

The psychological concept of the bystander effect, where individuals are less likely to take action in a group setting, can apply to cybersecurity incidents within organizations.

Employees may assume someone else will address a security issue, leading to delayed responses or inadequate mitigation efforts.

Cybersecurity professionals must consider the psychological aspects of incident response and ensure clear lines of responsibility and communication.

The psychology of trust is paramount in cybersecurity, as individuals and organizations rely on digital systems and services.

Trust in technology and online platforms can influence the willingness to share personal information and engage in online activities.

Trust can also be exploited by cybercriminals who impersonate trusted entities or create convincing fake websites.

Understanding the psychology of cybersecurity risk tolerance is crucial for organizations when making security-related decisions.

Balancing security measures with business objectives requires assessing and aligning risk tolerance across different stakeholders.

The psychology of cybersecurity extends to the design of user interfaces and security prompts.

Effective user interfaces should align with users' mental models, making security decisions clear and intuitive.

Security prompts should be well-timed and concise, avoiding information overload or decision fatigue.

In summary, the psychology of cybersecurity delves into the complex interplay between human behavior, cognition, and digital security.

Understanding how individuals perceive and interact with cybersecurity is essential for developing effective strategies to protect against cyber threats.

By addressing cognitive biases, promoting secure behaviors, and fostering a culture of cybersecurity awareness, individuals and organizations can enhance their defenses in an increasingly connected digital world.

Fostering a culture of cyber awareness is paramount in today's digitally driven world, where the constant evolution of technology brings both opportunities and risks.

Cyber threats are ubiquitous, and they can have far-reaching consequences, from financial losses to reputational damage and the compromise of sensitive information.

An organization's greatest defense against these threats lies not just in technology but also in its people.

A culture of cyber awareness empowers individuals at all levels of an organization to play an active role in safeguarding sensitive data and digital assets.

This culture begins with leadership, as executives and senior management must set the tone by demonstrating a commitment to cybersecurity.

When leaders prioritize cybersecurity, it sends a clear message to employees that protecting the organization's digital assets is a shared responsibility.

Furthermore, leaders must allocate the necessary resources and support for cybersecurity initiatives, ensuring that they have the tools and training needed to succeed.

Effective communication is a cornerstone of a culture of cyber awareness, as organizations must convey the importance of cybersecurity to all employees.

This communication should be ongoing, encompassing regular updates, reminders, and educational opportunities to keep cybersecurity top of mind.

Training programs play a pivotal role in building cyber awareness, as they provide employees with the knowledge and skills needed to recognize and respond to cyber threats.

Training should cover a range of topics, including phishing awareness, password security, and incident reporting procedures.

It's essential to make training engaging and relevant, tailoring content to employees' roles and responsibilities.

Simulated phishing exercises can be a valuable tool in training, allowing employees to practice identifying and avoiding phishing attempts in a controlled environment.

A culture of cyber awareness extends beyond the workplace, as individuals also need to protect themselves and their personal information online.

Organizations can provide guidance and resources to help employees practice good cybersecurity habits in their personal lives, reinforcing the importance of these behaviors.

Incentives and recognition can motivate employees to actively participate in cybersecurity efforts.

Acknowledging and rewarding individuals who demonstrate exemplary cyber awareness can encourage others to follow suit.

Creating a safe environment for reporting security incidents or concerns is vital in building trust between employees and the organization.

Employees should feel comfortable reporting incidents without fear of retribution, ensuring that potential threats are addressed promptly.

Cybersecurity policies and procedures should be accessible and easy to understand, providing clear guidance on how employees should handle various situations.

Regularly reviewing and updating these policies ensures that they remain relevant and effective in addressing evolving cyber threats.

Collaboration between different departments, such as IT, security, and HR, is essential for fostering a culture of cyber awareness.

These departments should work together to develop and implement cybersecurity initiatives that align with organizational goals.

Security champions or ambassadors can play a valuable role in promoting cyber awareness throughout an organization.

These individuals are passionate about cybersecurity and can help educate and inspire their colleagues.

Leadership should actively involve these champions in cybersecurity discussions and initiatives.

A culture of cyber awareness is not static; it evolves alongside technology and the threat landscape.

Organizations must adapt to new challenges by staying informed about emerging threats and technologies.

Regularly assessing the effectiveness of cybersecurity initiatives is crucial, allowing organizations to make improvements and adjustments as needed.

An incident response plan is an essential component of cyber awareness, as it outlines the steps to take when a cyber incident occurs.

Employees should be familiar with this plan and understand their roles and responsibilities in the event of a breach.

Collaboration with external partners and industry peers can provide valuable insights and threat intelligence that can help organizations stay ahead of cyber threats.

Promoting a culture of cyber awareness requires a collective effort, with everyone in the organization playing a part in protecting digital assets.

Ultimately, this culture becomes ingrained in the organization's DNA, shaping behaviors and decisions in a way that enhances security and resilience.

It is not a one-time initiative but an ongoing commitment to cybersecurity that adapts and evolves with the ever-changing digital landscape.

A strong culture of cyber awareness empowers organizations to mitigate risks, respond effectively to incidents, and maintain trust with stakeholders.

BOOK 2
MASTERING CYBERWATCH
ADVANCED TECHNIQUES FOR CYBERSECURITY
PROFESSIONALS
ROB BOTWRIGHT

Chapter 1: Advanced Threat Analysis and Intelligence

Understanding advanced cyber threats is essential in today's digital landscape, where the sophistication and frequency of attacks continue to rise.

These threats pose significant risks to individuals, organizations, and governments, and comprehending their nature is the first step in effective defense.

Advanced cyber threats encompass a wide range of malicious activities, from targeted attacks on specific individuals or organizations to large-scale campaigns with far-reaching consequences.

These threats often involve highly skilled attackers who employ advanced techniques and tools to achieve their objectives.

One prominent category of advanced cyber threats is Advanced Persistent Threats (APTs), which are long-term and stealthy campaigns conducted by well-funded and organized threat actors.

APTs typically focus on high-value targets, such as government agencies, critical infrastructure, or large enterprises, aiming to compromise their networks and exfiltrate sensitive information.

Advanced cyber threats often exploit zero-day vulnerabilities, which are previously unknown software vulnerabilities that have not yet been patched or fixed by the software vendor.

Attackers use these vulnerabilities to gain unauthorized access to systems and execute their malicious activities undetected.

Zero-day vulnerabilities are highly prized and can command significant prices on the black market or be reserved for targeted attacks.

Advanced cyber threats often employ sophisticated malware, such as rootkits, Trojans, or advanced persistent malware, specifically designed to evade detection and maintain persistence on compromised systems.

These malware variants often have advanced evasion techniques and can adapt to security measures, making them challenging to detect and mitigate.

Advanced cyber threats may also involve supply chain attacks, where attackers compromise software or hardware components at the source, leading to widespread vulnerabilities.

These attacks can be particularly challenging to detect, as they can compromise trusted vendors and introduce malicious code or vulnerabilities into legitimate products.

The motivations behind advanced cyber threats vary widely and may include espionage, financial gain, hacktivism, or state-sponsored activities.

Espionage-driven advanced threats focus on stealing sensitive information, intellectual property, or classified data for espionage purposes.

Financially motivated threats seek to compromise systems to steal financial data, conduct fraudulent transactions, or ransom data for monetary gain.

Hacktivism-driven threats are often politically motivated, aiming to disrupt or damage organizations or government entities to promote a specific cause or message.

State-sponsored threats are backed by nation-states or government agencies and target other nations or organizations to gather intelligence, conduct cyber espionage, or exert influence.

Advanced cyber threats often employ sophisticated tactics, techniques, and procedures (TTPs) to achieve their goals.

These TTPs include reconnaissance, where attackers gather information about their targets; weaponization, where malware or exploits are created or acquired; delivery, where the malicious payload is delivered to the target; exploitation, where vulnerabilities are exploited to gain access; and post-exploitation activities, where attackers establish persistence and move laterally within a network.

Detecting advanced cyber threats requires advanced security tools and technologies that can analyze network traffic, monitor system behavior, and detect anomalies that may indicate a breach.

Intrusion detection systems (IDS) and intrusion prevention systems (IPS) are essential components of advanced threat detection, as they can identify and block malicious activity in real-time.

Security information and event management (SIEM) solutions provide centralized logging and analysis of security events, helping organizations identify and respond to advanced threats.

Endpoint detection and response (EDR) solutions monitor and analyze the activities of endpoints, providing insight into potential breaches and allowing for rapid response.

Threat intelligence feeds and services provide up-to-date information about emerging threats and vulnerabilities, helping organizations proactively defend against advanced threats.

Machine learning and artificial intelligence (AI) play an increasingly important role in advanced threat detection, as they can analyze vast amounts of data to identify patterns and anomalies indicative of malicious activity.

Advanced cyber threats often employ social engineering techniques to manipulate individuals into revealing sensitive information or performing actions that benefit the attacker.

These techniques may include phishing emails, where attackers impersonate trusted entities to trick individuals into clicking on malicious links or providing login credentials.

Spear phishing targets specific individuals or organizations, often with personalized and convincing messages.

Whaling, a form of spear phishing, focuses on high-profile individuals, such as CEOs or government officials.

Vishing, or voice phishing, involves phone calls to extract sensitive information or manipulate individuals into taking specific actions.

Understanding the human element in advanced cyber threats is crucial, as it highlights the importance of cybersecurity awareness training for individuals within organizations.

Employees should be educated about the risks of social engineering and how to recognize and respond to suspicious communications.

Creating a security-aware culture within an organization can significantly reduce the success rate of social engineering attacks.

Advanced cyber threats are continuously evolving, making it essential for organizations to stay informed about emerging threats and vulnerabilities.

Regularly updating and patching software and systems can help mitigate the risk of falling victim to known vulnerabilities.

Penetration testing and vulnerability assessments can identify weaknesses that attackers could exploit, allowing organizations to proactively address them.

Collaboration with external security experts, information sharing organizations, and industry peers can provide valuable threat intelligence and insights into advanced cyber threats.

In summary, understanding advanced cyber threats is a critical aspect of modern cybersecurity.

These threats are diverse, sophisticated, and continuously evolving, posing significant risks to individuals and organizations.

To defend against advanced cyber threats, organizations must employ advanced security technologies, train employees in cybersecurity awareness, and stay informed about emerging threats and vulnerabilities.

A proactive and multi-layered approach to cybersecurity is essential in today's digital landscape.

Leveraging threat intelligence for proactive defense is a strategic approach that empowers organizations to stay one step ahead of cyber threats.

Threat intelligence involves the collection, analysis, and dissemination of information about potential cyber threats, attackers, and vulnerabilities.

This valuable information can be derived from a variety of sources, including open-source data, government agencies, security researchers, and industry-specific reports.

By harnessing threat intelligence, organizations can gain insights into emerging threats, attack techniques, and the motivations behind cyberattacks.

Proactive defense strategies rely on preemptive actions that aim to prevent cyberattacks before they occur.

One of the primary benefits of threat intelligence is its ability to provide organizations with early warnings about specific threats that may target their industry or sector.

For example, a financial institution can receive threat intelligence indicating a surge in banking Trojans or phishing campaigns targeting the financial sector.

Armed with this information, the organization can take proactive steps to fortify its defenses and educate employees about the specific threat.

Threat intelligence can be categorized into various types, including tactical, operational, and strategic intelligence.

Tactical threat intelligence focuses on specific indicators of compromise (IOCs), such as IP addresses, malware signatures, or malicious domains, which can be used to detect and block threats in real-time.

Operational threat intelligence provides insights into threat actors, their infrastructure, and tactics, techniques, and procedures (TTPs), allowing organizations to understand the broader context of cyber threats.

Strategic threat intelligence offers a high-level view of the threat landscape, helping organizations make informed decisions about long-term security investments and strategies.

The integration of threat intelligence into an organization's security infrastructure is crucial for proactive defense.

This integration involves collecting threat data, analyzing it for relevance and credibility, and applying it to enhance security measures.

Automated threat intelligence feeds can provide organizations with real-time updates on emerging threats and vulnerabilities, enabling immediate action.

Security information and event management (SIEM) systems can ingest threat intelligence data to correlate it with existing logs and generate alerts for potential threats.

Intrusion detection and prevention systems (IDS/IPS) can use threat intelligence feeds to block malicious traffic and enforce access controls.

Endpoint detection and response (EDR) solutions can benefit from threat intelligence by identifying and responding to threats on individual devices.

Threat intelligence platforms (TIPs) are dedicated tools that help organizations collect, aggregate, and analyze threat data from multiple sources.

TIPs provide a centralized repository for threat intelligence and facilitate collaboration among security teams.

Human analysis remains a critical component of leveraging threat intelligence effectively.

Security analysts play a pivotal role in evaluating the relevance and credibility of threat data, as well as adapting security measures accordingly.

By understanding the tactics, techniques, and procedures (TTPs) employed by threat actors, organizations can proactively adjust their security posture to counter specific threats.

Sharing threat intelligence within industry-specific Information Sharing and Analysis Centers (ISACs) or through formalized information-sharing agreements with peers can enhance collective defense efforts.

Collaborative threat intelligence sharing can help organizations benefit from the experiences and insights of others who may have encountered similar threats.

Government agencies, such as the Department of Homeland Security (DHS) in the United States, also provide threat intelligence information and guidance to help organizations protect critical infrastructure.

The Cyber Threat Intelligence Integration Center (CTIIC) within the Office of the Director of National Intelligence (ODNI) is another example of government initiatives aimed at sharing threat intelligence.

Threat intelligence can aid organizations in tracking and understanding the tactics of advanced persistent threats (APTs) and state-sponsored actors.

For example, threat intelligence may reveal patterns of behavior or indicators associated with nation-state-sponsored attacks.

With this information, organizations can tailor their defenses to detect and deter APTs more effectively.

Threat intelligence can also assist in identifying supply chain attacks, where attackers compromise software or hardware components at the source.

By monitoring threat intelligence feeds for information related to specific vendors or products, organizations can assess the risk of using those components in their infrastructure.

Understanding the motivations behind cyberattacks is another valuable aspect of threat intelligence.

Some threat actors are financially motivated, seeking to steal valuable data or extort organizations through ransomware attacks.

Others may be driven by ideology, hacktivism, or nation-state interests.

Knowing the motivations behind attacks can help organizations anticipate potential threats and tailor their defenses accordingly.

The proactive use of threat intelligence extends beyond technology and infrastructure.

It can inform decisions about security policies, risk assessments, and incident response plans.

For example, threat intelligence may reveal that a specific vulnerability is being actively exploited by threat actors.

In response, organizations can prioritize patching or mitigation efforts for that vulnerability.

Proactive defense strategies should also include ongoing employee education and training.

Employees can be a crucial line of defense against cyber threats, especially those involving social engineering.

Threat intelligence can inform security awareness programs, helping employees recognize and respond to specific threats relevant to their industry or region.

Threat intelligence should not be static but continuously updated and refined to reflect the evolving threat landscape.

Regularly reviewing and validating threat intelligence sources can help organizations ensure the accuracy and relevance of the data they rely on.

Collaboration with external cybersecurity experts, industry peers, and government agencies can provide valuable insights into emerging threats and vulnerabilities.

In summary, leveraging threat intelligence for proactive defense is a vital component of modern cybersecurity.

Organizations can use threat intelligence to stay ahead of emerging threats, tailor their defenses to specific risks, and make informed decisions about security investments and strategies.

By integrating threat intelligence into their security infrastructure, organizations can enhance their ability to detect, prevent, and respond to cyber threats proactively.

Chapter 2: Ethical Hacking and Penetration Testing

The role of ethical hackers in cybersecurity is indispensable, as they play a pivotal role in identifying vulnerabilities and strengthening an organization's defenses.

Ethical hackers, also known as white-hat hackers or penetration testers, are cybersecurity professionals who use their skills to uncover weaknesses in systems, applications, and networks.

Their work is crucial because it helps organizations identify and remediate vulnerabilities before malicious hackers can exploit them.

Ethical hackers follow a code of ethics and legal guidelines, ensuring that their activities are conducted with permission and within the bounds of the law.

Their primary objective is to improve security by identifying and addressing vulnerabilities, rather than causing harm or disruption.

One of the key roles of ethical hackers is conducting penetration tests, which involve simulating cyberattacks to assess the security posture of an organization's systems.

These tests help organizations identify vulnerabilities that could be exploited by malicious hackers and prioritize remediation efforts.

Ethical hackers use a variety of tools and techniques to assess an organization's security controls, such as network scanning, vulnerability assessment, and penetration testing.

They also conduct social engineering tests to assess the human element of security, including phishing simulations and physical security assessments.

Ethical hackers often work closely with an organization's security team to design and execute penetration tests that mimic real-world attack scenarios.

Their goal is to identify vulnerabilities that may not be apparent through automated scans and to assess the organization's ability to detect and respond to threats.

In addition to conducting penetration tests, ethical hackers also perform security assessments of applications, web services, and mobile apps.

They analyze the source code and configurations of these assets to identify vulnerabilities that could be exploited by attackers.

Ethical hackers may use manual code review, static analysis tools, and dynamic analysis techniques to uncover security weaknesses.

By identifying and remediating vulnerabilities in applications, ethical hackers help prevent data breaches, unauthorized access, and other security incidents.

Ethical hackers also play a role in red teaming exercises, where they simulate sophisticated cyberattacks to test an organization's overall security posture.

These exercises involve tactics, techniques, and procedures (TTPs) that closely resemble those used by real adversaries.

Red teaming helps organizations assess their readiness to defend against advanced threats and provides insights into potential weaknesses in their security defenses.

Ethical hackers are often involved in incident response and forensics, where they help investigate and analyze security incidents and breaches.

Their expertise in identifying attack vectors, malware analysis, and digital forensics can be invaluable in understanding the scope and impact of a cyber incident.

Ethical hackers can assist organizations in identifying the root cause of incidents, eradicating threats, and implementing measures to prevent future occurrences.

The role of ethical hackers extends to security research and the discovery of new vulnerabilities and exploits.

They often contribute to the security community by disclosing vulnerabilities responsibly to vendors, which enables timely patches and protects users.

Ethical hackers may also participate in bug bounty programs, where they are rewarded for identifying and responsibly disclosing security vulnerabilities.

These programs incentivize security researchers to proactively search for and report vulnerabilities in a responsible and ethical manner.

Ethical hackers are required to maintain a high level of expertise and stay up to date with the latest cybersecurity trends, techniques, and threats.

Certifications such as Certified Ethical Hacker (CEH) and Offensive Security Certified Professional (OSCP) are common credentials for ethical hackers, demonstrating their knowledge and skills in the field.

Ethical hackers must have a deep understanding of cybersecurity principles, network protocols, operating systems, and programming languages to effectively assess and secure systems.

In addition to technical skills, ethical hackers must possess strong problem-solving abilities, attention to detail, and creativity to identify novel attack vectors and vulnerabilities.

The collaboration between ethical hackers and organizations is crucial for maintaining robust cybersecurity defenses.

Organizations benefit from the expertise and insights of ethical hackers, who help identify and remediate vulnerabilities that could lead to security incidents.

Ethical hackers, in turn, gain valuable experience and contribute to the overall security of digital ecosystems.

The importance of ethical hacking in cybersecurity extends beyond the private sector; government agencies, critical infrastructure providers, and healthcare organizations also rely on ethical hackers to enhance their security posture.

The role of ethical hackers has evolved with the increasing complexity and sophistication of cyber threats.

Their work is essential for organizations seeking to protect sensitive data, maintain customer trust, and comply with regulatory requirements.

In summary, ethical hackers play a critical role in the cybersecurity landscape by proactively identifying and mitigating vulnerabilities, conducting penetration tests, assisting in incident response, and contributing to security research.

Their efforts help organizations bolster their defenses and stay ahead of evolving cyber threats, ultimately enhancing the security of digital environments.

Conducting effective penetration tests is a crucial component of modern cybersecurity strategies.

Penetration tests, often referred to as pen tests, are simulated cyberattacks designed to identify vulnerabilities and weaknesses in an organization's systems, applications, and networks.

These tests help organizations assess their security posture, uncover potential risks, and prioritize remediation efforts.

A successful penetration test not only identifies vulnerabilities but also provides actionable insights to improve security defenses.

The first step in conducting an effective penetration test is defining clear objectives and scope.

Organizations must determine what assets and systems will be tested, what types of attacks will be simulated, and what specific goals they want to achieve.

Having well-defined objectives ensures that the penetration test aligns with the organization's security goals and provides meaningful results.

Engaging experienced and qualified penetration testers is essential for a successful assessment.

Penetration testers should possess a deep understanding of cybersecurity principles, attack techniques, and the latest threats.

Certifications such as Certified Ethical Hacker (CEH) or Offensive Security Certified Professional (OSCP) can serve as indicators of a tester's knowledge and skills.

Choosing the right testing methodology is crucial, as different approaches may be appropriate for different scenarios.

Black-box testing, where testers have limited knowledge of the target systems, simulates attacks from external threat actors.

Gray-box testing provides testers with some knowledge of the target systems, mimicking attacks from insiders or privileged users.

White-box testing, on the other hand, provides testers with full access to system information and source code, allowing for a more comprehensive assessment.

Once the scope, objectives, and methodology are established, penetration testers begin the reconnaissance phase.

During this phase, testers gather information about the target environment, such as IP addresses, domain names, employee names, and organizational structure.

This information helps testers identify potential attack vectors and plan their approach.

Testers may use open-source intelligence (OSINT) techniques, such as searching publicly available information, to gather data about the target.

Vulnerability scanning and enumeration are critical steps in the penetration testing process.

Testers use automated tools to scan the target environment for known vulnerabilities and weaknesses.

This phase may involve port scanning, network discovery, and identifying software versions to pinpoint potential entry points.

Testers also enumerate user accounts, system configurations, and services to gather additional information for the attack.

The next phase of a penetration test involves exploiting vulnerabilities to gain unauthorized access or compromise systems.

Testers attempt to exploit the identified vulnerabilities while adhering to the rules of engagement defined in the scope.

Exploitation may involve using known exploits, custom-written code, or social engineering techniques to gain access.

Successful exploitation typically results in obtaining a foothold within the target environment.

Privilege escalation is a critical aspect of the penetration test, as it mimics an attacker's progression within a compromised system.

Testers attempt to elevate their privileges, moving from a standard user account to gain administrative or higher-level access.

Privilege escalation may involve exploiting misconfigurations, vulnerabilities, or weaknesses in access controls.

During the post-exploitation phase, testers assess the extent of control they have gained within the target environment.

They may pivot through the network, maintain persistence, and exfiltrate data to simulate the actions of a real attacker.

This phase helps organizations understand the potential impact of a successful cyberattack.

Effective communication is a key component of conducting penetration tests.

Testers should maintain ongoing communication with the organization's security team to provide updates on progress, findings, and potential risks.

Regular status reports and debriefings ensure that all stakeholders are informed and can take immediate action if necessary.

The final phase of a penetration test involves documenting the findings and delivering a comprehensive report to the organization.

The report should include detailed information about vulnerabilities, their impact, and recommended remediation steps.

The report should also prioritize vulnerabilities based on their severity and potential impact on the organization.

Organizations should use the penetration test report to prioritize and address vulnerabilities, update security policies, and improve security controls.

Conducting penetration tests regularly is essential to maintain a strong security posture.

Cyber threats are constantly evolving, and new vulnerabilities emerge regularly.

Regular testing helps organizations identify and remediate vulnerabilities before malicious actors can exploit them.

In addition to scheduled penetration tests, organizations should also consider conducting tests in response to significant changes in their environment, such as new software deployments or infrastructure changes.

External factors, such as emerging threats or industry-specific risks, may also warrant additional testing.

The role of penetration testing goes beyond identifying technical vulnerabilities; it also assesses the effectiveness of an organization's security policies, procedures, and incident response capabilities.

Penetration tests help organizations evaluate their readiness to detect, respond to, and recover from cyberattacks.

In summary, conducting effective penetration tests is a critical aspect of modern cybersecurity.

These tests help organizations identify vulnerabilities, assess their security posture, and prioritize remediation efforts.

By following a structured methodology, engaging experienced testers, and maintaining clear communication with stakeholders, organizations can enhance their security defenses and reduce the risk of cyberattacks.

Chapter 3: Intrusion Detection and Prevention Systems

Implementing intrusion detection systems (IDS) is a fundamental step in safeguarding an organization's digital assets against cyber threats.

IDS plays a vital role in monitoring network traffic, identifying suspicious activities, and detecting potential security breaches.

When effectively implemented, IDS can provide organizations with real-time alerts and insights into ongoing cyberattacks, allowing for timely response and mitigation.

The primary purpose of an IDS is to detect and respond to unauthorized or malicious activities within a network or system.

These activities can include intrusion attempts, malware infections, insider threats, and other forms of cyberattacks.

An IDS works by analyzing network traffic and system logs for patterns or anomalies that indicate potential security incidents.

There are two main types of IDS: network-based intrusion detection systems (NIDS) and host-based intrusion detection systems (HIDS).

NIDS monitors network traffic at the network perimeter, inspecting packets for suspicious patterns and signatures.

HIDS, on the other hand, focuses on individual host systems, analyzing system logs, file integrity, and system configurations for signs of compromise.

Implementing NIDS involves strategically placing sensors or sniffers at key points within the network architecture.

These sensors capture network traffic and send it to the NIDS engine for analysis.

The NIDS engine employs various detection techniques, such as signature-based detection, anomaly-based detection, and heuristic analysis, to identify potential threats.

Signature-based detection relies on a predefined database of known attack signatures or patterns.

When network traffic matches a known signature, the NIDS generates an alert.

Anomaly-based detection, on the other hand, establishes a baseline of normal network behavior and alerts on deviations from this baseline.

Heuristic analysis involves the use of algorithms to identify suspicious behaviors or patterns that may not be covered by signatures.

HIDS, on the other hand, is implemented on individual host systems, such as servers, workstations, and endpoints.

HIDS agents are installed on these systems to monitor and analyze system activities and events.

HIDS agents can detect unauthorized access, changes to critical files, and suspicious processes running on host systems.

When implementing HIDS, organizations should carefully configure and tune the agents to minimize false positives and ensure efficient operation.

The effectiveness of an IDS relies on continuous monitoring, analysis, and alerting.

To implement an IDS successfully, organizations must consider several key factors.

Firstly, organizations should define the scope and objectives of the IDS implementation.

This includes identifying the assets to be protected, the types of threats to be detected, and the network segments or host systems to be monitored.

Clear objectives help organizations tailor the IDS to their specific security requirements.

Selecting the right IDS solution is a critical decision in the implementation process.

Organizations should choose an IDS that aligns with their infrastructure, network architecture, and security goals.

Considerations include whether to implement a commercial IDS solution, open-source IDS software, or a combination of both.

Additionally, organizations should evaluate the scalability and performance of the IDS solution to ensure it can meet their current and future needs.

The next step in implementing an IDS is designing the network or host-based sensors or agents.

Placement is crucial to ensure comprehensive coverage while minimizing performance overhead.

NIDS sensors should be strategically positioned at key network chokepoints, such as entry and exit points, data centers, and critical network segments.

HIDS agents should be installed on all relevant host systems, including servers, workstations, and critical endpoints.

Once sensors or agents are deployed, organizations must configure and fine-tune the IDS to minimize false positives and optimize detection accuracy.

This involves defining and customizing alerting thresholds, adjusting signature or detection rules, and configuring event correlation.

Additionally, organizations should establish response and escalation procedures for handling IDS alerts.

This includes defining roles and responsibilities for incident response, specifying escalation paths, and establishing incident severity levels.

The effectiveness of an IDS implementation relies on real-time alerting and incident response capabilities.

Organizations should ensure that IDS alerts are promptly reviewed by trained security personnel who can assess the severity of the alert and take appropriate action.

This may involve verifying the alert, investigating the incident, isolating affected systems, and applying necessary remediation measures.

Organizations should also integrate their IDS with a Security Information and Event Management (SIEM) system or other central logging and analysis tools.

SIEM integration enables correlation of IDS alerts with other security events, providing a more comprehensive view of the threat landscape.

Additionally, organizations can use SIEM solutions to store and analyze historical data, aiding in incident forensics and compliance reporting.

Continuous monitoring and regular IDS maintenance are essential components of a successful implementation.

Organizations should routinely update IDS signatures, rules, and detection mechanisms to stay ahead of emerging threats.

Regular software updates and security patches should be applied to the IDS solution itself to mitigate potential vulnerabilities.

Furthermore, organizations should conduct periodic reviews and assessments of their IDS configurations and rules to ensure they remain aligned with evolving security requirements.

IDS logs and alerts should be retained and archived for compliance, auditing, and incident investigation purposes.

Organizations should establish a robust log retention policy that aligns with regulatory requirements and internal security standards.

In summary, implementing intrusion detection systems (IDS) is a critical component of a comprehensive cybersecurity strategy.

IDS plays a crucial role in monitoring network and host activities, identifying security threats, and facilitating timely incident response.

By carefully planning the scope, selecting the right solution, strategically placing sensors or agents, and maintaining a proactive approach to monitoring and tuning, organizations can leverage IDS to enhance their overall security posture and protect against evolving cyber threats.

Proactive threat mitigation with intrusion prevention systems (IPS) is a vital aspect of modern cybersecurity strategies.

IPS solutions are designed to identify and block potential threats before they can infiltrate an organization's network or compromise its systems.

By actively monitoring network traffic and applying security policies and rules, IPS plays a crucial role in preventing malicious activities and safeguarding an organization's digital assets.

The primary objective of an IPS is to detect and prevent unauthorized access, data breaches, malware infections, and other security incidents.

IPS solutions employ a range of techniques, including signature-based detection, anomaly-based detection, and stateful packet inspection, to identify and thwart potential threats.

Signature-based detection relies on a database of known attack signatures or patterns, allowing the IPS to detect and block attacks that match these predefined signatures.

Anomaly-based detection focuses on identifying abnormal or suspicious patterns of network traffic that deviate from established baselines.

Stateful packet inspection, or deep packet inspection, analyzes the content and context of network packets to detect and block malicious activities.

Implementing an IPS requires careful planning and consideration of an organization's specific security requirements.

Organizations should define the scope and objectives of IPS deployment, identifying the assets and systems to be protected and the types of threats to be mitigated.

The choice of an IPS solution should align with the organization's infrastructure, network architecture, and security goals.

Factors such as scalability, performance, and ease of management should also be considered when selecting an IPS solution.

The next step in proactive threat mitigation with IPS is designing and configuring the system for optimal effectiveness.

This includes defining and customizing security policies, rules, and filters based on the organization's security requirements.

IPS rules should be tailored to address known vulnerabilities and emerging threats, and they should be regularly updated to stay current.

Organizations should establish clear policies for incident response and escalation procedures when the IPS detects and blocks suspicious activities.

This involves defining roles and responsibilities, specifying response actions, and establishing incident severity levels.

To ensure the effective operation of an IPS, organizations should regularly update the system with the latest signatures, patches, and firmware updates.

IPS solutions often rely on a subscription-based service to receive updates for new threats and vulnerabilities.

Organizations should also conduct regular performance and configuration assessments of their IPS to verify that it is operating optimally.

Effective monitoring and alerting are essential for proactive threat mitigation with IPS.

Organizations should ensure that alerts generated by the IPS are promptly reviewed by trained security personnel who can assess the severity of the alert and take appropriate action.

This may involve investigating the incident, isolating affected systems, and applying remediation measures.

Intrusion prevention systems should be integrated with other security technologies, such as intrusion detection systems (IDS), firewalls, and security information and event management (SIEM) solutions.

Integration allows for enhanced threat visibility, correlation of security events, and centralized management.

Regularly reviewing and analyzing IPS logs and alerts can provide valuable insights into the threat landscape and aid in incident forensics.

Organizations should also consider conducting periodic penetration tests and vulnerability assessments to evaluate the effectiveness of their IPS in mitigating threats.

In addition to real-time threat prevention, IPS solutions can provide organizations with historical data and reporting capabilities.

This data can be valuable for compliance, auditing, and reporting purposes.

Organizations should establish a robust log retention policy that aligns with regulatory requirements and internal security standards.

In summary, proactive threat mitigation with intrusion prevention systems (IPS) is an essential component of modern cybersecurity strategies.

IPS plays a critical role in identifying and preventing potential threats, protecting an organization's digital assets, and safeguarding its reputation.

By carefully planning the scope, selecting the right solution, configuring policies and rules, establishing incident response procedures, and ensuring continuous monitoring and updates, organizations can leverage IPS to enhance their overall security posture and defend against evolving cyber threats.

Chapter 4: Advanced Cryptography and Encryption

Cryptographic protocols for advanced security are fundamental tools in the field of cybersecurity, providing the foundation for secure communication, data protection, and authentication.

These protocols leverage mathematical techniques to ensure the confidentiality, integrity, and authenticity of digital information in an increasingly interconnected and digitized world.

One of the most widely used cryptographic protocols is the Secure Sockets Layer (SSL) or its successor, the Transport Layer Security (TLS) protocol, which are essential for securing communication over the internet.

SSL and TLS protocols establish encrypted connections between web browsers and servers, ensuring that data exchanged during online transactions remains confidential and tamper-proof.

They employ a combination of symmetric and asymmetric encryption to protect data in transit, making it extremely difficult for unauthorized parties to eavesdrop or intercept sensitive information.

Beyond secure communication, cryptographic protocols play a vital role in user authentication and access control.

The Password Authentication Protocol (PAP), Challenge Handshake Authentication Protocol (CHAP), and Extensible Authentication Protocol (EAP) are examples of cryptographic protocols used to verify the identity of users and devices.

These protocols help prevent unauthorized access to systems and resources, ensuring that only authenticated and authorized individuals or entities can gain access.

Cryptographic protocols also support the establishment of secure virtual private networks (VPNs), which allow organizations to create encrypted tunnels for data transmission over public networks.

The Point-to-Point Tunneling Protocol (PPTP), Layer 2 Tunneling Protocol (L2TP), and Internet Protocol Security (IPsec) are cryptographic protocols commonly used in VPNs to provide secure, private communication between remote locations.

Additionally, cryptographic protocols are indispensable in digital signatures and certificate management.

The Public Key Infrastructure (PKI) relies on cryptographic protocols to issue, revoke, and validate digital certificates, which are used to verify the authenticity and integrity of digital documents and communications.

Digital signatures, created using protocols like the Digital Signature Algorithm (DSA) or the RSA algorithm, provide a means to ensure the origin and integrity of electronic messages and transactions.

Cryptographic protocols also enable secure email communication through the Pretty Good Privacy (PGP) and Secure/Multipurpose Internet Mail Extensions (S/MIME) protocols, which use encryption and digital signatures to protect the confidentiality and authenticity of email messages.

In the realm of secure file storage and sharing, cryptographic protocols such as the Secure/Multipurpose Internet Mail Extensions (S/MIME) protocols play a crucial role in securing data both at rest and in transit.

Protocols like the Secure File Transfer Protocol (SFTP) and the Secure Shell (SSH) protocol ensure secure file transfers and remote access to servers, safeguarding sensitive information from unauthorized access and tampering.

Furthermore, cryptographic protocols are integral to blockchain technology, which underpins cryptocurrencies like Bitcoin and Ethereum.

The blockchain uses cryptographic algorithms and protocols to secure transactions, create digital wallets, and establish consensus among network participants, ensuring the integrity and immutability of the ledger.

Modern cryptographic protocols must also address the emerging challenges of quantum computing, which threatens the security of existing cryptographic algorithms.

Post-quantum cryptography research is underway to develop new protocols that can withstand the computational power of quantum computers, ensuring long-term security for digital systems.

Cryptographic protocols are not without their challenges, including the need for continuous updates and improvements to stay ahead of evolving threats.

The cryptographic community collaborates to address vulnerabilities and weaknesses in existing protocols and develop stronger encryption algorithms and methods.

Interoperability and standardization are also important considerations, as different organizations and systems must be able to communicate securely using compatible protocols.

To ensure the successful implementation of cryptographic protocols, organizations must establish robust key management practices, including key generation, distribution, storage, and revocation.

Without proper key management, the security provided by cryptographic protocols can be compromised.

Furthermore, organizations must educate their personnel on the importance of following security best practices and not compromising the confidentiality and integrity of cryptographic keys.

In summary, cryptographic protocols are the bedrock of advanced security in the digital age, providing essential tools for secure communication, data protection, authentication, and access control.

These protocols play a vital role in safeguarding sensitive information, enabling secure online transactions, and ensuring the integrity of digital systems.

As technology continues to evolve and threats become more sophisticated, cryptographic protocols must adapt and improve to meet the ever-changing demands of cybersecurity.

Encrypting data at rest and in transit is a critical aspect of modern cybersecurity, providing a robust layer of protection against unauthorized access and data breaches.

Data encryption is the process of converting plain-text data into an unreadable format, known as ciphertext, using cryptographic algorithms and keys.

Encrypting data at rest involves securing information that is stored on various devices and storage media, such as hard drives, databases, and cloud storage.

This ensures that even if an attacker gains physical access to the storage device, they cannot decipher the data without the encryption key.

Encrypting data in transit, on the other hand, focuses on securing information as it is transmitted over networks, whether they are wired or wireless.

This safeguards data from interception or tampering while in transit, making it unreadable to unauthorized parties.

One of the most commonly used encryption protocols for securing data in transit is the Secure Sockets Layer (SSL) or its successor, the Transport Layer Security (TLS) protocol.

These protocols establish secure connections between clients (such as web browsers) and servers, ensuring that data exchanged during online transactions remains confidential and protected from eavesdropping.

To implement data encryption at rest, organizations use encryption algorithms and cryptographic keys to transform sensitive data before storing it on various storage media.

Encryption keys play a central role in this process, as they are used to both encrypt and decrypt the data.

There are two primary types of encryption: symmetric encryption and asymmetric encryption.

Symmetric encryption uses the same key for both encryption and decryption, making it faster and efficient for encrypting large volumes of data.

However, it requires secure key management to ensure that the encryption key is not compromised.

In contrast, asymmetric encryption uses a pair of keys: a public key for encryption and a private key for decryption.

This approach offers enhanced security, as the private key must be kept confidential, but it is typically slower than symmetric encryption.

When encrypting data at rest, organizations must consider various factors, including selecting the appropriate encryption algorithm, key length, and encryption mode.

Encryption algorithms, such as Advanced Encryption Standard (AES) and Triple Data Encryption Standard (3DES), provide varying levels of security and performance.

Organizations should choose algorithms and key lengths based on their security requirements and the sensitivity of the data being protected.

Additionally, the mode of encryption, such as Cipher Block Chaining (CBC) or Electronic Codebook (ECB), affects how data is encrypted and should be chosen based on specific use cases.

Secure key management is crucial for the success of data encryption at rest.

Organizations must implement strong key management practices, including key generation, distribution, storage, rotation, and disposal.

Encryption keys should be protected from unauthorized access and regularly rotated to mitigate risks associated with long-term key exposure.

To ensure the effectiveness of data encryption at rest, organizations should also consider implementing access controls and authentication mechanisms to prevent unauthorized users from accessing encrypted data.

This includes user authentication, role-based access control, and robust auditing to track and monitor data access.

Encrypting data in transit is equally important, especially in an era of widespread data transmission over networks.

To secure data during transmission, organizations rely on encryption protocols like SSL/TLS, which use a combination of symmetric and asymmetric encryption to establish secure connections.

When a user or client initiates a connection to a server, a handshake process occurs, during which the server presents its digital certificate and public key to the client.

The client and server then exchange symmetric encryption keys, which are used to encrypt and decrypt data during the session.

The encryption keys are unique to each session, providing a high level of security.

Encrypting data in transit is essential for securing online transactions, sensitive communications, and remote access to systems.

Organizations must ensure that encryption protocols are correctly configured and that digital certificates are issued and managed securely to prevent man-in-the-middle attacks and other vulnerabilities.

Encrypting data at rest and in transit helps organizations comply with regulatory requirements and industry standards related to data protection and privacy.

Encryption is often a mandatory component of data security regulations, such as the General Data Protection Regulation (GDPR) in Europe and the Health Insurance Portability and Accountability Act (HIPAA) in the healthcare industry.

Failure to implement encryption can result in non-compliance and potential legal consequences.

Encryption also provides a layer of defense against data breaches and cyberattacks.

Even if an attacker gains unauthorized access to a storage device or intercepts data in transit, the encrypted data remains unreadable without the encryption keys.

This helps mitigate the impact of data breaches and limits the exposure of sensitive information.

In summary, encrypting data at rest and in transit is a fundamental cybersecurity practice that protects sensitive information from unauthorized access and data breaches.

Encryption ensures that data remains confidential and secure, even when stored on devices or transmitted over networks.

Organizations must carefully select encryption algorithms, key management practices, and security controls to effectively implement data encryption and maintain compliance with regulatory requirements.

Chapter 5: Secure Network Architecture and Design

Designing resilient and secure networks is a complex and critical task in the field of information technology, as the interconnected nature of modern systems demands robust protection against cyber threats and the ability to withstand unexpected disruptions.

Resilience and security go hand in hand, as a network that is resilient is better equipped to withstand and recover from security incidents. A resilient network can continue to function even in the face of network breaches or hardware failures, minimizing downtime and data loss.

To achieve this level of resilience and security, network architects and administrators must carefully plan, implement, and manage a range of security measures and strategies.

At the core of designing resilient and secure networks is the concept of defense in depth, which involves layering security controls and mechanisms to create multiple lines of defense.

This approach ensures that even if one layer is breached, others remain in place to mitigate the impact of the attack.

One fundamental aspect of network resilience and security is the segmentation of the network into distinct security zones or segments. Segmentation helps contain potential breaches, limiting the lateral movement of attackers within the network.

Organizations typically employ techniques such as virtual LANs (VLANs), firewalls, and access control lists (ACLs) to establish network segmentation.

Additionally, network architects must consider the principle of least privilege when designing network access controls.

Users and devices should only be granted the minimum level of access necessary to perform their tasks, reducing the attack surface and limiting the potential impact of a breach.

Access controls, including authentication and authorization mechanisms, play a crucial role in enforcing the principle of least privilege.

Authentication ensures that users and devices are who they claim to be, while authorization determines what resources and services they are allowed to access.

Network administrators should implement strong authentication methods, such as multi-factor authentication (MFA), to enhance security.

Furthermore, they must regularly review and update access control lists and policies to reflect changes in the network's topology and user requirements.

Another key component of designing resilient and secure networks is the use of encryption to protect data in transit and at rest.

Encryption algorithms and protocols, such as the Transport Layer Security (TLS) and Advanced Encryption Standard (AES), ensure that data remains confidential and protected from eavesdropping and unauthorized access.

Network architects must carefully select encryption mechanisms based on the sensitivity of the data being transmitted or stored.

Encryption should be employed for all sensitive communications, including email, file transfers, and remote access.

Security Information and Event Management (SIEM) systems are valuable tools for network resilience and security.

SIEM solutions provide real-time monitoring, analysis, and correlation of security events and incidents within the network.

They help organizations detect and respond to security threats quickly and effectively.

By aggregating data from various network devices and security controls, SIEM systems provide a holistic view of the network's security posture.

Organizations can use SIEM solutions to identify patterns of behavior indicative of security breaches, enabling proactive response.

Additionally, SIEM systems assist in compliance reporting by generating detailed logs and reports of security events and incidents.

Resilient and secure networks must also incorporate regular vulnerability assessments and penetration testing to identify and remediate weaknesses.

Vulnerability assessments involve scanning the network for known vulnerabilities and misconfigurations, providing a baseline for security improvements.

Penetration testing, on the other hand, simulates real-world attacks to evaluate the effectiveness of security controls and discover potential weaknesses.

These assessments help organizations prioritize remediation efforts and ensure that the network remains resilient against emerging threats.

Network administrators should stay informed about current threats and vulnerabilities by monitoring security advisories and patches released by software vendors and security organizations.

Regularly applying security updates and patches is essential to mitigate known vulnerabilities and protect the network from exploitation.

Additionally, network administrators should implement a robust incident response plan to address security incidents effectively.

This plan should include defined roles and responsibilities, incident severity levels, communication protocols, and predefined response actions.

Regular training and drills can help ensure that the incident response team is well-prepared to handle security incidents and minimize their impact.

Resilience and security also extend to the physical layer of the network infrastructure. Data centers and critical network components should be housed in secure facilities with appropriate access controls, environmental safeguards, and redundancy to withstand physical threats and disasters.

Furthermore, organizations should implement backup and disaster recovery plans to ensure data availability and business continuity in case of unexpected disruptions.

These plans should include offsite backups, failover mechanisms, and regular testing to validate their effectiveness.

Network architects and administrators must also be vigilant about insider threats, as trusted individuals within the organization can pose a significant risk to network security.

User education and awareness programs can help employees recognize and report suspicious activities, reducing the likelihood of insider threats.

To enhance network resilience and security, organizations should also consider implementing security information sharing and threat intelligence programs.

These programs allow organizations to collaborate with peers and security experts to share threat intelligence and stay informed about emerging threats. In summary, designing resilient and secure networks is a multifaceted endeavor that requires careful planning, layered security controls, ongoing monitoring, and proactive response capabilities.

By following best practices and employing a defense-in-depth approach, organizations can create networks that are robust, adaptive, and resilient in the face of evolving cyber threats and unforeseen disruptions. Network segmentation is a crucial strategy for enhancing security in modern IT environments, as it involves dividing a network into smaller, isolated segments or zones to minimize attack surface and contain potential breaches.

This approach recognizes that not all parts of a network require the same level of access or security.

By dividing the network into segments based on factors such as function, user groups, or sensitivity of data, organizations can implement security controls more effectively and reduce the risk of lateral movement by attackers.

Network segmentation provides an additional layer of defense by preventing unauthorized access to critical resources and limiting the impact of security incidents.

In essence, it creates virtual boundaries within the network, separating different parts to ensure that a breach in one area does not automatically compromise the entire network.

One common method of network segmentation is through the use of VLANs, or Virtual Local Area Networks.

VLANs allow network administrators to group devices into separate logical networks, even if they are physically connected to the same network infrastructure.

This separation is achieved by assigning devices to different VLANs and configuring network switches to isolate traffic between these VLANs.

For example, an organization might have separate VLANs for employees, guests, and sensitive servers, ensuring that these groups cannot communicate directly with each other unless explicitly permitted.

Another method of network segmentation is through the use of firewalls and access control lists (ACLs).

Firewalls act as gatekeepers between network segments, filtering traffic based on predefined rules and policies.

Access control lists are used to define what traffic is allowed or denied between segments.

Firewalls and ACLs are valuable tools for enforcing security policies and controlling communication between different parts of the network.

Furthermore, network segmentation is essential for ensuring compliance with regulatory requirements and industry standards.

Many regulations, such as the Payment Card Industry Data Security Standard (PCI DSS) and the Health Insurance Portability and Accountability Act (HIPAA), mandate the implementation of network segmentation to protect sensitive data.

Segmenting the network helps organizations demonstrate compliance by isolating cardholder data or personal health information from other parts of the network.

Additionally, network segmentation can improve network performance and resource utilization.

By isolating traffic and dedicating specific resources to each segment, organizations can optimize network bandwidth and reduce congestion.

This can lead to improved application performance and overall network efficiency.

Network segmentation also facilitates easier troubleshooting and network management.

When an issue arises within a specific segment, it can be isolated and addressed without affecting the rest of the network.

This simplifies problem resolution and reduces downtime.

Implementing network segmentation requires careful planning and consideration of the organization's specific requirements and objectives.

First, organizations must define the segmentation strategy by identifying the segments they want to create and the criteria for segmenting devices or users.

This may involve classifying devices based on their function, sensitivity, or location.

Next, organizations must select the appropriate segmentation technology and tools.

For VLAN-based segmentation, network switches with VLAN support are necessary.

For firewall-based segmentation, organizations should choose firewalls that align with their security policies and requirements.

Once the segmentation technology is in place, organizations must configure the network devices and security controls to enforce the segmentation.

This involves assigning devices to specific VLANs, configuring firewall rules, and defining ACLs.

Security policies should be established to govern traffic flow between segments, specifying which devices or users are allowed to communicate with each other.

Regular monitoring and auditing of the segmentation are crucial to ensure that security controls are effective and that there are no misconfigurations or policy violations.

Network administrators should review and update segmentation rules as needed to accommodate changes in the network environment.

Additionally, organizations should consider implementing intrusion detection and prevention systems (IDS/IPS) to monitor traffic between segments and detect potential security threats or anomalies.

IDS/IPS solutions can provide real-time alerts and block malicious traffic, enhancing the security of segmented networks.

In summary, network segmentation is a fundamental strategy for enhancing security, compliance, and performance in modern IT environments.

It involves dividing a network into smaller, isolated segments to minimize the attack surface, control access, and contain potential breaches.

By carefully planning and implementing segmentation strategies, organizations can strengthen their overall security posture and protect critical resources from unauthorized access or compromise.

Chapter 6: Incident Response and Forensics

Building an effective incident response plan is a critical aspect of modern cybersecurity, as organizations face an ever-evolving landscape of cyber threats and security breaches.

An incident response plan is a structured approach to addressing and mitigating security incidents, ensuring that organizations can respond promptly and effectively when breaches or security events occur.

The primary goal of an incident response plan is to minimize the impact of incidents, reduce downtime, protect sensitive data, and maintain the organization's reputation.

A well-designed incident response plan defines roles, responsibilities, procedures, and communication protocols for handling security incidents.

The plan should be comprehensive and cover a wide range of incident types, including but not limited to data breaches, malware infections, denial-of-service attacks, and insider threats.

The incident response team plays a crucial role in executing the plan, and it typically consists of members from various departments, including IT, legal, communications, and management.

One of the first steps in building an effective incident response plan is identifying the assets and data that need protection.

Organizations should conduct a thorough inventory of their digital assets, including servers, databases, applications, and sensitive information.

Understanding what needs protection is essential for prioritizing incident response efforts.

Next, organizations should define the criticality of these assets and data, categorizing them based on their importance to the business.

This criticality assessment helps determine the level of response and recovery efforts required for each asset.

Incident classification is another crucial component of the plan, as it ensures that incidents are categorized correctly, allowing for the appropriate response measures.

Incident classification can be based on severity, impact, or type of incident, and it guides the incident response team's actions.

Once incidents are classified, organizations should establish a clear incident notification and reporting process.

This process outlines how employees, partners, or customers can report incidents, ensuring that potential security threats are quickly identified and addressed.

The incident response plan should include specific procedures for containing and isolating security incidents to prevent further damage or unauthorized access.

This involves actions such as disconnecting compromised systems from the network, shutting down affected services, or blocking malicious traffic.

Incident containment is critical for limiting the extent of an incident and preventing its spread throughout the organization.

After containment, organizations should focus on eradicating the root cause of the incident.

This may involve identifying and removing malware, patching vulnerabilities, or addressing misconfigurations that allowed the incident to occur.

Once the incident is eradicated, organizations should implement recovery procedures to restore affected systems and services to normal operation.

These procedures should be well-documented and tested to ensure a swift recovery process.

The incident response plan should also detail how organizations communicate with internal and external stakeholders during and after an incident.

This includes notifying employees, customers, partners, regulatory authorities, and the public, if necessary.

Effective communication is essential for managing the reputation and trust of the organization.

Legal and compliance considerations are significant factors in incident response planning.

Organizations should be aware of legal requirements and regulations that may apply to specific incidents, such as data breach notification laws.

The incident response plan should address compliance requirements and outline how the organization will adhere to them during an incident.

Regular training and awareness programs are essential for ensuring that employees understand their roles and responsibilities within the incident response plan.

Training helps the incident response team and other staff members effectively execute their roles during a security incident.

Additionally, organizations should conduct tabletop exercises and simulations to test the effectiveness of the incident response plan.

These exercises help identify weaknesses, improve coordination, and refine the plan based on real-world scenarios.

Regularly reviewing and updating the incident response plan is crucial to ensure that it remains effective in the face of evolving threats.

As new threats and attack techniques emerge, organizations must adapt their incident response strategies accordingly.

The incident response plan should be a living document that is continuously improved and refined.

Organizations should also establish key performance indicators (KPIs) and metrics to assess the effectiveness of their incident response efforts.

KPIs can include metrics such as incident detection and response times, incident resolution rates, and the number of incidents successfully contained.

These metrics provide insights into the organization's incident response capabilities and help identify areas for improvement.

In summary, building an effective incident response plan is essential for organizations to effectively mitigate the impact of security incidents and protect their digital assets and reputation.

A well-designed plan outlines procedures, roles, responsibilities, and communication protocols for addressing a wide range of incidents.

Regular training, testing, and continuous improvement are key elements of maintaining an effective incident response program in the ever-changing landscape of cybersecurity threats.

Digital forensics techniques play a crucial role in cyber investigations, as they enable investigators to uncover, analyze, and preserve digital evidence related to cybercrimes and security incidents.

These techniques encompass a wide range of processes and tools that help collect and examine data from various digital sources, including computers, mobile devices, network logs, and cloud services.

The ultimate goal of digital forensics is to identify and attribute cyber threats, gather evidence for legal proceedings, and enhance overall cybersecurity.

One of the primary digital forensics techniques is the acquisition of digital evidence, which involves creating a copy or image of a digital device or storage medium without altering the original data.

This process ensures the integrity of the evidence and allows investigators to work with a duplicate while preserving the original state for analysis and legal purposes.

Imaging tools and hardware write blockers are commonly used in this phase to ensure that the evidence remains unchanged during acquisition.

Once the evidence is acquired, investigators employ data recovery techniques to retrieve deleted or hidden information that may be relevant to the investigation.

This involves examining file systems, analyzing unallocated space, and using specialized software to recover deleted files and fragments.

Data carving is a technique used to search for specific file signatures or patterns within the acquired data, allowing investigators to extract files even if file system metadata is missing or damaged.

Keyword searches and file signature analysis are integral to data carving.

Digital forensics experts often encounter encrypted data during their investigations, requiring the use of decryption techniques to access protected information.

Decryption may involve cracking passwords, recovering encryption keys, or bypassing encryption protections to reveal the underlying content.

Cryptography experts and specialized software are essential in these efforts to ensure the security and integrity of the process.

Timeline analysis is a valuable technique in digital forensics, enabling investigators to reconstruct the sequence of events leading up to and during a cyber incident.

This involves examining timestamps, logs, and system artifacts to create a chronological timeline of activities and interactions within the digital environment.

Timeline analysis can provide critical insights into the progression of an incident and help identify its origin and impact.

Malware analysis is a specialized digital forensics technique used to examine malicious software and identify its behavior, functionality, and purpose.

Reverse engineering is often employed to dissect and analyze malware samples to understand their inner workings and assess potential vulnerabilities or weaknesses.

Static analysis and dynamic analysis are common approaches in malware analysis, offering insights into the code structure and behavior of malicious software.

Network forensics techniques focus on the analysis of network traffic and communication patterns to investigate cyber incidents and intrusions.

Packet capture and analysis tools are used to collect data from network segments and analyze the flow of information.

Investigators examine network logs, packet headers, and payload data to identify anomalies, unauthorized access, or suspicious activities.

Steganography detection is a digital forensics technique used to uncover hidden messages or data concealed within digital files.

Steganography tools and algorithms embed information within seemingly innocuous files, such as images or audio files.

To detect hidden data, investigators employ steganalysis techniques that analyze file structures and pixel values to identify anomalies.

Mobile device forensics is a specialized branch of digital forensics focused on collecting and analyzing data from smartphones, tablets, and other mobile devices.

Investigators use mobile device forensics tools to extract call logs, text messages, emails, app data, and geolocation information.

Cloud forensics techniques are essential for investigating cybercrimes and security incidents involving cloud services and storage.

Investigators access cloud service APIs and analyze logs and metadata to trace data access, sharing, and modification.

Cloud forensics also involves obtaining legal authorization to access cloud data and ensuring the chain of custody is maintained.

Volatility analysis is a digital forensics technique used to examine the volatile memory (RAM) of a computer or device.

Volatile memory may contain valuable information related to running processes, active network connections, encryption keys, and more.

Investigators use volatility analysis tools to capture and analyze RAM contents, providing insights into the state of the system at the time of the incident.

Chain of custody documentation is a fundamental aspect of digital forensics, ensuring the integrity and admissibility of evidence in legal proceedings.

Investigators meticulously record the handling, storage, and transfer of digital evidence to maintain a clear and unbroken chain of custody.

Legal considerations and compliance with evidence preservation protocols are essential in this phase.

Expert testimony and reporting are vital components of digital forensics, as investigators often provide expert witness testimony in court.

Investigators must prepare comprehensive reports detailing their findings, methodologies, and conclusions to support legal proceedings.

The ability to communicate complex technical information clearly and effectively is essential in presenting evidence to judges and juries.

In summary, digital forensics techniques are essential tools for cyber investigations, allowing investigators to collect, analyze, and preserve digital evidence related to cybercrimes and security incidents.

These techniques encompass a wide range of processes and tools, from data acquisition and recovery to timeline analysis, malware analysis, and network forensics.

Digital forensics experts must adhere to legal and ethical standards while providing expert testimony and maintaining the chain of custody to ensure the integrity and admissibility of evidence in legal proceedings.

Chapter 7: Security Automation and Orchestration

Streamlining security operations with automation is a transformative approach in the field of cybersecurity, as it leverages technology to enhance the efficiency and effectiveness of security tasks and processes.

Automation involves the use of software, scripts, and algorithms to perform routine and repetitive security tasks without human intervention, allowing security teams to focus on more strategic and complex aspects of their roles.

One of the key benefits of automation in security operations is its ability to significantly reduce response times to security incidents.

Automated incident detection and alerting systems can identify and respond to threats in real-time, ensuring that security teams are alerted promptly when suspicious activities occur.

This rapid response helps mitigate the impact of incidents and minimizes potential damage.

Another advantage of automation is its ability to improve accuracy and consistency in security operations.

Human errors can occur when performing manual tasks, such as analyzing logs or configuring security policies, but automation eliminates these errors by executing tasks consistently and according to predefined rules.

Automation also enables organizations to enforce security policies and configurations uniformly across their entire infrastructure.

Security policies can be encoded as scripts or configurations that are automatically applied to all relevant systems, ensuring compliance and reducing the risk of misconfigurations.

Furthermore, automation can enhance threat intelligence by continuously collecting, analyzing, and disseminating information about emerging threats and vulnerabilities.

Automated threat intelligence feeds and integrations with security tools enable organizations to stay updated on the latest security risks and take proactive measures to protect their systems.

Automation also plays a crucial role in vulnerability management by automatically scanning and assessing systems for vulnerabilities.

Vulnerability scanning tools can identify weaknesses in software, operating systems, and configurations, enabling security teams to prioritize and remediate vulnerabilities more effectively.

Patch management is another area where automation can streamline security operations.

Automated patch management systems can deploy security updates and patches to vulnerable systems promptly, reducing the window of opportunity for attackers to exploit known vulnerabilities.

Security orchestration and automation platforms (SOAR) are specialized tools that facilitate the automation of complex security workflows.

These platforms allow security teams to create custom automation playbooks that integrate with various security tools and technologies.

For example, a SOAR platform can automate the investigation and response to phishing incidents by collecting email headers, analyzing attachments, and blocking malicious domains or IPs.

Additionally, automation can enhance incident response by providing automated playbooks for common incident types.

These playbooks guide security analysts through predefined steps and actions to contain, investigate, and remediate incidents efficiently.

Automation can also facilitate the sharing of threat intelligence and incident data with external organizations and industry peers through standardized formats and protocols.

Security information sharing platforms and automated feeds enable organizations to collaborate in real-time, strengthening collective defenses against cyber threats.

Intrusion detection and prevention systems (IDS/IPS) benefit from automation by allowing automated rule updates and responses to emerging threats.

Automated blocking of malicious traffic or IP addresses based on threat intelligence feeds can proactively protect the network from known threats.

Security automation extends beyond traditional IT environments to include cloud security.

Cloud security posture management (CSPM) tools leverage automation to continuously assess cloud configurations for misconfigurations and compliance violations.

These tools provide recommendations and automate remediation actions to secure cloud resources effectively.

Network security automation involves the use of tools and technologies to automatically configure and manage security devices, such as firewalls and routers.

Automation can update access control lists (ACLs), implement firewall rules, and monitor network traffic for anomalies, reducing the manual effort required for network security.

Security information and event management (SIEM) systems benefit from automation by automatically correlating and analyzing security events, reducing the volume of alerts and false positives that analysts need to review.

Machine learning algorithms can automate threat detection and provide insights into anomalous behavior patterns.

Automation can also enhance threat hunting by using advanced analytics to identify potential threats and indicators of compromise (IoCs).

Automated threat hunting tools can continuously analyze large datasets and uncover hidden threats that might go unnoticed with manual analysis.

Moreover, automation can help organizations achieve compliance with regulatory requirements and industry standards.

Automated compliance checks and reporting can demonstrate adherence to security policies and regulations, reducing the administrative burden of compliance audits.

The automation of security awareness training and phishing simulations can educate employees and reduce the likelihood of falling victim to social engineering attacks.

Security automation is not without challenges, and organizations must consider factors such as false positives, false negatives, and the potential for automation to perpetuate biases or errors present in the initial rule sets.

Therefore, it is essential to continuously monitor and fine-tune automated security systems to ensure their effectiveness.

Additionally, organizations should invest in the training and development of security professionals with expertise in automation technologies.

In summary, streamlining security operations with automation is a powerful approach that enhances the efficiency, accuracy, and effectiveness of cybersecurity efforts.

Automation can expedite incident response, improve threat intelligence, facilitate vulnerability management, and enforce security policies consistently across an organization's infrastructure.

By leveraging automation, organizations can better protect their digital assets and respond to cyber threats with agility and precision in today's rapidly evolving threat landscape.

Orchestration for efficient incident response represents a strategic approach in the realm of cybersecurity, offering organizations the means to streamline and optimize their incident handling processes.

This approach leverages automation and coordination to enhance the speed, consistency, and effectiveness of incident response actions.

The core concept of orchestration revolves around the automation of manual tasks and the synchronization of various security tools and technologies, creating a well-orchestrated incident response workflow.

The primary goal of incident response orchestration is to reduce the mean time to respond (MTTR) to security incidents, ultimately minimizing the impact and damage caused by cyberattacks.

In an era of increasingly sophisticated and frequent cyber threats, rapid response is essential to safeguarding an organization's digital assets and maintaining business continuity.

Orchestration allows security teams to harness the power of automation to execute predefined incident response actions swiftly.

By automating repetitive and time-consuming tasks, such as data enrichment, containment, and evidence gathering, security professionals can allocate more time to strategic decision-making and threat hunting.

Moreover, orchestration ensures that incident response procedures are executed consistently across the organization, reducing the risk of errors or omissions during high-stress situations.

This consistency not only enhances security but also aids in compliance with regulatory requirements, as organizations can demonstrate a structured and repeatable incident response process.

Central to the orchestration approach is the use of playbooks, which are sets of predefined steps and actions that guide incident responders through the various stages of an incident.

Playbooks encompass a wide range of actions, from simple tasks like isolating a compromised device to complex processes involving threat analysis, containment, and eradication.

These playbooks are created and customized to align with an organization's specific incident response procedures and security policies.

Playbooks serve as a blueprint for orchestrating incident response, ensuring that every incident is handled consistently and efficiently.

Orchestration platforms or security orchestration, automation, and response (SOAR) solutions play a pivotal role in incident response orchestration.

These platforms serve as the central hub for managing and executing playbooks, integrating with various security tools, and orchestrating incident response actions.

SOAR platforms provide a unified interface for incident responders to view and manage incidents, initiate automated actions, and collaborate effectively.

Integration capabilities are a cornerstone of incident response orchestration, allowing organizations to connect and coordinate their existing security technologies seamlessly.

Integration with security information and event management (SIEM) systems, threat intelligence feeds, endpoint detection and response (EDR) solutions, and network security tools ensures that incident responders have access to real-time data and contextual information.

This enables them to make informed decisions and take immediate action in response to threats.

Furthermore, incident response orchestration can incorporate threat intelligence feeds and indicators of compromise (IoCs) to enrich incident data and automate the identification of malicious activities.

By automatically cross-referencing incoming incident data with threat intelligence, organizations can swiftly identify known threats and respond accordingly.

Incident prioritization is another critical aspect of orchestration, as it allows organizations to assign severity levels to incidents and prioritize their response efforts accordingly.

Automated incident triage can assess the potential impact and urgency of an incident, enabling security teams to allocate resources based on the level of risk posed.

For example, incidents involving critical systems or sensitive data may receive a higher priority, triggering immediate containment and investigation actions.

Incident communication and collaboration are streamlined through orchestration platforms, which facilitate communication between incident responders, IT teams, legal, and other stakeholders.

Secure chat, incident timelines, and task assignment capabilities ensure that incident response activities are coordinated effectively, even in complex and distributed environments.

Automation of communication tasks, such as notifying affected parties and regulatory authorities, helps organizations maintain transparency and meet legal obligations.

Orchestration platforms also offer reporting and analytics capabilities that allow organizations to assess their incident response performance.

Metrics, such as MTTR, incident volume, and incident resolution rates, provide valuable insights into the efficiency and effectiveness of incident response operations.

These metrics help organizations identify areas for improvement and make data-driven decisions to enhance their incident response capabilities continually.

Despite the numerous benefits of incident response orchestration, it is essential to acknowledge potential challenges and considerations.

Organizations must invest time in designing and implementing effective playbooks that align with their specific needs and procedures.

Additionally, incident response orchestration requires continuous monitoring and refinement to ensure that automated actions and playbooks remain effective against evolving threats.

Organizations should also consider the integration of artificial intelligence (AI) and machine learning (ML) capabilities into their orchestration platforms to further enhance threat detection and response.

In summary, orchestration for efficient incident response is a strategic approach that empowers organizations to optimize their incident handling processes through automation and coordination.

By leveraging orchestration platforms and customized playbooks, organizations can accelerate incident response, enhance consistency, and reduce the impact of cyber threats.

Integration with existing security technologies, threat intelligence feeds, and incident prioritization capabilities ensures that organizations are well-equipped to respond effectively to the ever-evolving threat landscape.

Ultimately, incident response orchestration is a cornerstone of modern cybersecurity, enabling organizations to defend against cyberattacks with agility and precision.

Chapter 8: Cloud Security Strategies

Securing cloud environments and workloads is of paramount importance in the modern digital landscape, as organizations increasingly rely on cloud services and platforms to power their operations.

The cloud offers undeniable advantages in terms of scalability, flexibility, and cost-efficiency, but it also presents unique security challenges that must be addressed comprehensively.

The shared responsibility model is a fundamental concept in cloud security, as it delineates the division of security responsibilities between cloud service providers (CSPs) and cloud customers.

CSPs are responsible for securing the underlying cloud infrastructure, such as the physical data centers, networking, and hypervisors.

Cloud customers, on the other hand, are responsible for securing their workloads, applications, data, and access to cloud resources.

Understanding this division of responsibilities is crucial for cloud customers to implement effective security measures within their cloud environments.

Identity and access management (IAM) is a foundational aspect of cloud security, as controlling and managing access to cloud resources is paramount.

IAM solutions enable organizations to define and enforce granular access policies, ensuring that only authorized users and entities can interact with cloud resources.

Multi-factor authentication (MFA) is a critical component of IAM, providing an additional layer of security by requiring users to authenticate their identity through multiple methods.

Strong authentication mechanisms, such as biometrics or hardware tokens, enhance access security.

Encryption is a fundamental security control that should be applied consistently in cloud environments to protect data at rest and in transit.

Data encryption ensures that even if unauthorized access occurs, the data remains unintelligible without the appropriate decryption keys.

Organizations should implement encryption for sensitive data stored in cloud databases, file storage, and during data transmission between cloud services.

Cloud security posture management (CSPM) tools play a pivotal role in assessing and maintaining the security of cloud environments.

These tools continuously monitor cloud configurations for misconfigurations, compliance violations, and security weaknesses.

CSPM solutions provide organizations with real-time insights into the state of their cloud security and offer remediation recommendations to mitigate risks.

Vulnerability management is essential in cloud security to identify and remediate security vulnerabilities that could be exploited by attackers.

Regular vulnerability scanning of cloud instances, virtual machines, and containerized workloads helps organizations maintain a secure cloud posture.

Security patching and updates should be applied promptly to address known vulnerabilities and prevent exploitation.

Container security is a critical consideration for organizations using containerization technologies in the cloud.

Containers can introduce security challenges if not properly configured and secured.

Implementing container security best practices, such as restricting container privileges, scanning container images for vulnerabilities, and monitoring container behavior, is essential for securing cloud workloads.

Network security in the cloud requires a holistic approach, encompassing virtual private clouds (VPCs), security groups, and network access controls.

Organizations should define network segmentation strategies to isolate workloads and limit lateral movement in case of a breach.

Intrusion detection and prevention systems (IDS/IPS) should be deployed to monitor network traffic for suspicious activities and block malicious traffic.

Cloud workload protection platforms (CWPP) provide additional layers of security for cloud workloads, including runtime protection, behavioral analysis, and threat detection.

These platforms help organizations detect and respond to threats targeting cloud-based applications and workloads.

Logging and monitoring are indispensable for cloud security, as they provide visibility into cloud activity and enable the detection of security incidents and anomalies.

Cloud-native security information and event management (SIEM) solutions collect and analyze logs from cloud services, enabling rapid incident response and forensic analysis.

Security information sharing and collaboration are essential aspects of cloud security, as organizations can benefit from collective threat intelligence and best practices.

Participating in cloud security alliances and sharing threat indicators with peers can enhance security posture.

Compliance with industry-specific regulations and data protection laws is a crucial consideration for organizations using cloud services.

Cloud customers must ensure that their cloud deployments adhere to relevant compliance requirements, such as the General Data Protection Regulation (GDPR) or the Health Insurance Portability and Accountability Act (HIPAA).

Incident response planning is essential for cloud security, as organizations must be prepared to respond effectively to security incidents and data breaches.

Cloud-specific incident response playbooks and procedures should be developed, tested, and integrated into the organization's overall incident response plan.

Security awareness and training programs should include cloud security best practices, ensuring that employees are aware of the unique security considerations associated with cloud usage. Cloud security certifications and training for cloud security professionals can enhance an organization's expertise in securing cloud environments.

Third-party security assessments and penetration testing can help organizations identify and address vulnerabilities and weaknesses in their cloud deployments.

In summary, securing cloud environments and workloads is a multifaceted endeavor that requires a comprehensive approach encompassing identity and access management, encryption, security posture management, vulnerability management, network security, container security, and logging and monitoring.

Organizations must embrace a shared responsibility model, leverage cloud security tools, and prioritize compliance, incident response, and security awareness to mitigate the unique security challenges posed by cloud adoption.

By addressing these challenges proactively and holistically, organizations can harness the benefits of the cloud while maintaining a robust security posture in an ever-evolving threat landscape. Cloud Identity and Access Management (IAM) is a critical component of cloud security, as it governs how users and entities are granted access to cloud resources and services.

IAM encompasses a set of policies, processes, and technologies that enable organizations to control and manage user identities, authentication, authorization, and permissions within their cloud environments.

Central to cloud IAM is the concept of identity, which represents a unique digital representation of an individual, device, application, or service.

Identities are assigned and managed within an organization's identity provider (IdP) and are used to verify the authenticity of users and entities attempting to access cloud resources.

Authentication is the process of verifying the identity of users and entities, typically through a combination of usernames and passwords, security tokens, or biometric authentication methods.

Multi-factor authentication (MFA) enhances the security of authentication by requiring users to provide two or more forms of verification, such as something they know (password), something they have (security token), or something they are (biometric data).

Once authenticated, users and entities are authorized based on their roles, permissions, and access policies defined in the cloud IAM system.

Authorization determines what actions and resources users and entities are allowed to access within the cloud environment.

Role-based access control (RBAC) is a common authorization model in cloud IAM, where users are assigned to roles that dictate their level of access to specific resources and services.

Fine-grained access controls allow organizations to specify precise permissions for users and entities, ensuring that access is limited to what is necessary for their roles.

Cloud IAM systems provide a centralized location for organizations to manage and enforce access policies across their cloud infrastructure.

This centralized control simplifies the management of access permissions and reduces the risk of inconsistent or incorrect access settings.

Identity federation is a key feature of cloud IAM, enabling organizations to establish trust relationships between their on-premises IdP and cloud IdP to facilitate single sign-on (SSO) experiences for users.

SSO allows users to log in once and access multiple cloud services without the need to re-enter credentials.

Cloud IAM also extends to the management of external identities, such as customers, partners, and vendors, through the use of identity providers or identity federation.

Identity federation can also be used to provide controlled access to external users while maintaining security and auditability.

Identity lifecycle management is an essential aspect of cloud IAM, as it ensures that user identities are created, modified, and deactivated in accordance with organizational policies and compliance requirements.

Automated provisioning and deprovisioning processes help organizations efficiently manage user identities throughout their lifecycle.

User self-service features empower users to reset passwords, update profile information, and request access to additional resources without involving IT support.

Audit and logging capabilities are integral to cloud IAM, enabling organizations to monitor and track user activities and access to resources.

Audit logs provide visibility into authentication and authorization events, helping organizations detect suspicious or unauthorized activities.

Security information and event management (SIEM) solutions can ingest and analyze IAM logs to detect anomalies and security incidents.

Identity governance and compliance management are critical components of cloud IAM, helping organizations maintain compliance with regulatory requirements and internal policies.

Automated identity certification processes allow organizations to periodically review and validate users' access rights, ensuring that they align with their roles and responsibilities.

Cloud IAM systems also provide reporting and auditing features that facilitate compliance audits and reporting to regulatory bodies.

In the context of cloud IAM, privilege escalation is a significant security concern, as attackers may attempt to gain unauthorized access to privileged accounts with elevated permissions.

To mitigate this risk, organizations should implement strong access controls and monitor for suspicious activity associated with privileged accounts.

Cloud IAM solutions offer the capability to enforce password policies, password rotation, and password complexity requirements to enhance security.

Additionally, organizations can implement identity and access management policies that enforce the principle of least privilege (PoLP), ensuring that users and entities have only the minimum necessary access to perform their tasks.

User and entity behavior analytics (UEBA) can complement cloud IAM by monitoring and analyzing patterns of user and entity behavior to detect unusual or potentially malicious activities.

UEBA can identify insider threats and external attacks that may evade traditional security measures.

In summary, cloud Identity and Access Management (IAM) is a foundational component of cloud security that governs the authentication, authorization, and management of user identities and entities within cloud environments.

IAM controls access to cloud resources, enforces security policies, and ensures compliance with regulatory requirements.

Key components of cloud IAM include authentication, authorization, role-based access control, identity federation, lifecycle management, audit and logging, identity governance, and compliance management.

Organizations must implement robust cloud IAM practices and solutions to safeguard their cloud assets and protect against security threats and unauthorized access.

Chapter 9: IoT Security Challenges and Solutions

Understanding IoT security risks is essential in today's interconnected world, where the Internet of Things (IoT) has become a ubiquitous part of our daily lives, permeating various industries and applications.

IoT devices, which include everything from smart home appliances to industrial sensors, bring unprecedented convenience and efficiency, but they also introduce a wide range of security vulnerabilities and risks.

One of the primary security concerns with IoT devices is their sheer number and diversity, making them an attractive target for cybercriminals.

The proliferation of IoT devices means that organizations and individuals must manage a complex and rapidly expanding attack surface, where each device potentially represents a point of entry for malicious actors.

Many IoT devices are resource-constrained, lacking the processing power and memory to implement robust security measures, which makes them susceptible to exploitation.

In addition to this, IoT devices often have long lifespans and may not receive regular security updates, leaving them vulnerable to known vulnerabilities that are left unpatched for extended periods.

IoT devices are commonly deployed in remote or uncontrolled environments, which can make physical security difficult to maintain, exposing them to tampering, theft, and unauthorized access.

Furthermore, IoT devices often communicate wirelessly, relying on protocols like Wi-Fi, Bluetooth, Zigbee, or cellular networks, which can be susceptible to eavesdropping and interception.

The data generated and transmitted by IoT devices can be highly sensitive, encompassing personal information, industrial process data, and critical infrastructure control signals.

If not adequately protected, this data can be intercepted or manipulated, leading to privacy breaches, industrial espionage, or even physical harm.

Manufacturers of IoT devices often prioritize functionality and cost-effectiveness over security during product development, resulting in devices with inadequate security features and default passwords that are rarely changed by end-users.

The use of default or easily guessable passwords represents a significant security risk, as attackers can gain unauthorized access to devices and compromise them.

IoT devices are typically designed for ease of use and convenience, which often results in simplified user interfaces and limited security controls.

This lack of security configurability can hinder users' ability to implement proper security measures, such as disabling unnecessary features or applying access controls.

IoT devices are frequently interconnected and share data with other devices or cloud-based services, creating complex ecosystems of interdependencies.

Weaknesses in one device or component can propagate security vulnerabilities throughout the entire ecosystem, potentially leading to cascading security breaches.

Additionally, the communication and data exchange between devices can introduce new attack vectors, allowing attackers to exploit vulnerabilities in one device to compromise others within the same network.

IoT devices are often managed and controlled remotely through web interfaces or mobile apps, which can be vulnerable to web application attacks, such as cross-site scripting (XSS) or SQL injection.

If these management interfaces lack proper security controls, attackers can manipulate them to gain unauthorized access or control over IoT devices.

The supply chain for IoT devices is complex and can involve multiple vendors, making it challenging to ensure the security of all components and software embedded in a device.

Malicious actors may target vulnerabilities in third-party software or hardware components to compromise IoT devices at different stages of the supply chain.

The proliferation of IoT devices in critical infrastructure sectors, such as energy, healthcare, and transportation, introduces the potential for severe consequences if these devices are compromised.

Attacks on IoT devices within critical infrastructure can disrupt essential services, cause physical harm, or compromise national security.

The unique challenges presented by IoT security require organizations and individuals to adopt a proactive and comprehensive approach to mitigating risks.

Effective IoT security begins with robust device authentication and access controls, ensuring that only authorized entities can interact with IoT devices and their data.

Authentication mechanisms should go beyond basic passwords and incorporate stronger forms of authentication, such as two-factor authentication (2FA) or biometric authentication.

IoT device manufacturers should prioritize security by design, implementing security features and best practices during the development process.

This includes secure boot processes, regular security updates, and the removal of default or hardcoded passwords.

Organizations should establish thorough security policies and practices for deploying and managing IoT devices, including inventory management, vulnerability assessments, and incident response procedures.

Network segmentation is a critical security measure that can isolate IoT devices from critical systems and limit the potential impact of a compromise.

By segregating IoT devices into separate network segments, organizations can reduce the attack surface and contain security incidents.

Encryption is fundamental in protecting data transmitted between IoT devices and backend systems, ensuring that even if intercepted, the data remains confidential and secure.

Security monitoring and threat detection mechanisms should be in place to identify anomalous behavior or security incidents involving IoT devices.

Machine learning and artificial intelligence can be leveraged to analyze large volumes of IoT data and identify patterns indicative of security threats.

Regular security audits and penetration testing can help organizations identify vulnerabilities in their IoT deployments and validate the effectiveness of their security controls.

Security awareness and training programs should be extended to cover IoT security best practices for both end-users and IT personnel.

Legal and regulatory frameworks, such as the General Data Protection Regulation (GDPR) and the California Consumer Privacy Act (CCPA), are increasingly addressing IoT security and privacy concerns, imposing obligations on organizations to protect user data and disclose security incidents.

In summary, understanding IoT security risks is crucial in a world where IoT devices are becoming an integral part of our personal and professional lives.

While these devices offer numerous benefits, they also introduce a wide range of security challenges that must be addressed proactively.

IoT security requires a holistic approach encompassing device security, network security, data protection, supply chain security, and security best practices throughout the device lifecycle.

By adopting comprehensive security measures, organizations and individuals can harness the benefits of IoT while minimizing the associated security risks.

Implementing security measures for IoT devices is an essential step in protecting the integrity, confidentiality, and availability of these interconnected devices in an increasingly connected world.

IoT devices, ranging from smart thermostats and wearable fitness trackers to industrial sensors and medical devices, have proliferated across various sectors and industries, offering convenience, automation, and improved efficiency.

However, the widespread adoption of IoT has also brought forth significant security challenges that organizations and individuals must address proactively.

One of the foundational principles of securing IoT devices is to establish robust authentication mechanisms, ensuring that only authorized users and entities can access and interact with the devices.

Authentication can take various forms, including passwords, cryptographic keys, biometrics, or two-factor authentication (2FA), with the choice depending on the device's capabilities and use case.

Strong and unique passwords or cryptographic keys should be enforced to prevent unauthorized access and the use of default or easily guessable credentials.

Secure boot processes play a crucial role in ensuring the integrity of IoT device firmware and software.

During the boot-up sequence, the device should verify the authenticity and integrity of the software components, ensuring that they have not been tampered with or compromised.

Regularly updating and patching IoT device firmware is essential to address known vulnerabilities and security issues.

Device manufacturers should provide timely and easy-to-apply updates to ensure that devices remain secure throughout their lifecycle.

Network security is another critical aspect of IoT security, as devices often communicate wirelessly through various protocols like Wi-Fi, Bluetooth, Zigbee, or cellular networks.

Implementing encryption for data transmitted between devices and backend systems is imperative to protect sensitive information from interception or tampering.

Additionally, network segmentation can isolate IoT devices from critical systems, reducing the attack surface and limiting potential lateral movement in case of a security breach.

Securing the IoT ecosystem also involves managing the identities and permissions of users and entities that interact with devices.

Role-based access control (RBAC) allows organizations to define and enforce access policies, ensuring that individuals or entities have the appropriate level of access to specific resources based on their roles and responsibilities.

IoT devices often rely on cloud services for data storage, processing, and remote management.

Therefore, securing cloud interactions and data storage is integral to IoT security.

Organizations should ensure that cloud providers implement robust security measures, such as encryption at rest and in transit, access controls, and regular security assessments.

Data privacy is a significant concern in the context of IoT, as these devices collect and transmit vast amounts of personal and sensitive data.

Implementing privacy-by-design principles and adhering to data protection regulations, such as the General Data Protection Regulation (GDPR) or the California Consumer Privacy Act (CCPA), is essential to protect user privacy.

Physical security measures must not be overlooked, especially for IoT devices deployed in remote or uncontrolled environments.

Protecting devices from physical tampering, theft, or unauthorized access is critical to maintaining their security.

This can include measures such as tamper-evident seals, secure enclosures, and access controls to device physical interfaces.

Supply chain security is another important consideration, as IoT devices are often composed of multiple components from various vendors.

Organizations should conduct thorough security assessments of the supply chain to identify and mitigate potential risks at different stages, from component manufacturing to device assembly.

Implementing a robust incident response plan is crucial for IoT security, as it enables organizations to respond swiftly and effectively to security incidents and data breaches.

This plan should encompass processes for identifying, containing, mitigating, and recovering from security breaches while ensuring compliance with regulatory reporting requirements.

Security awareness and training programs are essential for both end-users and IT personnel to educate them about IoT security risks and best practices.

Users should be made aware of their responsibilities in ensuring the security of IoT devices, such as changing default passwords, updating firmware, and recognizing potential security threats.

IoT device manufacturers play a pivotal role in improving IoT security by incorporating security measures into their products from the design phase.

This includes conducting security assessments and penetration testing, eliminating hardcoded or default passwords, providing secure update mechanisms, and supporting responsible disclosure of vulnerabilities.

Regulatory bodies and industry organizations are increasingly addressing IoT security concerns by developing standards, guidelines, and best practices for manufacturers and users alike.

These initiatives aim to establish a baseline for IoT security, encouraging the adoption of secure design and operational practices.

In summary, implementing security measures for IoT devices is crucial in safeguarding these interconnected devices from various threats and vulnerabilities.

IoT security requires a multifaceted approach encompassing authentication, secure boot processes, firmware updates, network security, access controls, cloud security, data privacy, physical security, supply chain security, incident response, and security awareness.

By adopting these security measures and considering security throughout the entire lifecycle of IoT devices, organizations and individuals can leverage the benefits of IoT while minimizing associated security risks.

Chapter 10: Emerging Threats and Future Trends in Cybersecurity

Exploring the evolving cyber threat landscape is a critical endeavor in today's interconnected digital world, as the threat landscape constantly evolves in response to technological advancements, new attack vectors, and changing attacker tactics.

The digital realm has become an integral part of our daily lives, with individuals, businesses, and governments relying on technology for communication, commerce, and critical infrastructure.

However, this increasing dependence on technology has also made us more susceptible to cyber threats, as malicious actors seek to exploit vulnerabilities for financial gain, political motives, or simply to create chaos.

One of the notable trends in the evolving cyber threat landscape is the growing sophistication of cybercriminals and state-sponsored actors.

These adversaries have access to advanced tools, techniques, and resources, enabling them to carry out highly targeted and complex attacks.

Sophisticated threat actors often conduct extensive reconnaissance and employ custom malware designed to evade detection, making their activities challenging to identify and mitigate.

Another prominent aspect of the evolving threat landscape is the rise of ransomware attacks, where cybercriminals encrypt victims' data and demand a ransom for its release.

Ransomware attacks have become more prevalent and financially lucrative, with attackers increasingly targeting critical infrastructure, healthcare organizations, and government entities.

The impact of ransomware attacks extends beyond financial losses, as they can disrupt essential services, compromise sensitive data, and erode public trust.

In recent years, supply chain attacks have gained notoriety as a potent method for compromising multiple organizations through a single attack vector.

Supply chain attacks involve infiltrating a trusted vendor's or supplier's network and using it as a platform to target the vendor's customers.

This technique allows threat actors to compromise numerous organizations downstream, potentially exposing sensitive data and undermining the security of an entire ecosystem.

Nation-state actors have been actively engaged in cyber espionage and cyber-attacks on a global scale.

These state-sponsored threats often target government institutions, critical infrastructure, and private-sector organizations, with the goal of advancing political or strategic objectives.

Cyber-espionage campaigns may involve the theft of sensitive government secrets, intellectual property, or research data.

Furthermore, disinformation campaigns and cyber-attacks on election systems have become prominent tools for influencing political events and undermining democratic processes.

The Internet of Things (IoT) has introduced a new dimension to the evolving threat landscape, as the proliferation of IoT devices presents numerous security challenges.

Many IoT devices lack robust security features, making them susceptible to compromise.

Attackers have exploited vulnerabilities in IoT devices to create massive botnets for launching distributed denial-of-service (DDoS) attacks, which can disrupt online services and websites.

Moreover, IoT devices often collect and transmit sensitive data, raising concerns about privacy and data security.

The growing interconnectedness of critical infrastructure, such as power grids, water treatment plants, and transportation systems, has made them attractive targets for cyberattacks.

Disrupting critical infrastructure can have severe consequences, including power outages, transportation disruptions, and public safety risks.

Cyber-attacks on critical infrastructure have the potential to cause physical harm and economic damage.

The advent of 5G technology brings both opportunities and security challenges.

While 5G promises faster and more reliable connectivity, it also introduces new attack vectors, such as increased attack surface due to a greater number of connected devices and the potential for attacks on the 5G infrastructure itself.

The proliferation of mobile devices and remote work arrangements has expanded the attack surface for cybercriminals.

Remote work introduces additional security concerns, as employees access corporate networks from potentially less secure home environments.

Phishing attacks and social engineering techniques have become more sophisticated, with attackers crafting convincing emails and messages to deceive users into revealing sensitive information or downloading malware.

Cybercriminals also exploit global events and crises, such as the COVID-19 pandemic, by launching phishing campaigns related to health information, vaccine distribution, and remote work.

The underground cybercrime economy has continued to thrive, with cybercriminals offering a range of services, including malware-as-a-service (MaaS), ransomware-as-a-service (RaaS), and hacking tools for sale on the dark web.

These services enable less technically proficient individuals to engage in cybercrime, widening the pool of potential threat actors.

The evolving threat landscape necessitates a proactive and multi-faceted approach to cybersecurity.

Organizations and individuals must continuously assess and enhance their security measures to mitigate the risks posed by evolving threats.

This includes implementing robust cybersecurity practices, regularly updating and patching systems and software, conducting security awareness training, and investing in advanced threat detection and response capabilities.

Collaboration and information sharing among organizations and the cybersecurity community are essential for identifying emerging threats and vulnerabilities.

Government agencies, law enforcement, and private-sector organizations must work together to combat cyber threats effectively.

Moreover, international cooperation is crucial to addressing threats originating from foreign adversaries and state-sponsored actors.

In summary, exploring the evolving cyber threat landscape is vital for understanding the dynamic and complex nature of modern cybersecurity challenges.

The digital age has brought numerous benefits, but it has also exposed us to an ever-changing array of cyber threats, from sophisticated nation-state actors to ransomware operators and IoT vulnerabilities.

By staying informed, adopting best practices, and collaborating with others, we can better protect our digital assets and defend against the evolving threats that confront us in the digital era.

Preparing for future cybersecurity challenges is essential as the digital landscape continues to evolve at a rapid pace, introducing new threats and vulnerabilities.

Cybersecurity is an ever-changing field, and staying ahead of emerging threats requires a proactive and adaptive approach.

The first step in preparing for future cybersecurity challenges is to recognize that the threat landscape is constantly evolving, driven by advancements in technology, changes in attacker tactics, and shifts in the geopolitical landscape.

Organizations and individuals must accept that cybersecurity is an ongoing process and that there is no one-size-fits-all solution.

One of the key challenges in preparing for future cybersecurity threats is the increasing complexity of IT environments.

As organizations embrace cloud computing, mobile devices, IoT, and 5G technology, the attack surface expands, creating more opportunities for cybercriminals to exploit vulnerabilities.

To address this complexity, organizations must implement comprehensive security strategies that cover all aspects of their digital infrastructure.

Another major challenge is the growing sophistication of cyberattacks, with threat actors using advanced techniques and tools to breach defenses.

In response, cybersecurity professionals must continually upgrade their skills and knowledge to detect and mitigate these evolving threats effectively.

Machine learning and artificial intelligence are becoming essential tools in the fight against cybercrime, helping organizations analyze vast amounts of data to identify patterns indicative of malicious activity.

Cybersecurity professionals must embrace these technologies to keep pace with adversaries.

Cybersecurity awareness and training programs are also crucial in preparing for future challenges.

End-users are often the weakest link in the security chain, as they can inadvertently fall victim to phishing attacks, social engineering, or other forms of deception.

Education and training can empower individuals to recognize and report potential threats, enhancing overall security.

The integration of cybersecurity into organizational culture is another essential aspect of preparation.

Cybersecurity should not be an isolated function within an organization but an integral part of its DNA.

This involves establishing a cybersecurity culture that emphasizes the importance of security at all levels and across all departments.

Collaboration and information sharing among organizations and within the cybersecurity community are vital for preparing for future challenges.

Threat intelligence sharing helps organizations stay informed about emerging threats and vulnerabilities.

Government agencies, private-sector organizations, and international partners must work together to tackle global cyber threats effectively.

The regulatory landscape is also evolving, with governments worldwide introducing data protection and privacy laws.

Organizations must stay compliant with these regulations and ensure that their cybersecurity practices align with legal requirements.

In addition to external threats, organizations must also consider insider threats, which can be just as damaging.

Malicious insiders or negligent employees can compromise data and systems, making it essential to implement access controls, monitoring, and auditing to detect and prevent insider threats.

The increasing connectivity of critical infrastructure and the adoption of IoT devices in critical sectors pose unique challenges in terms of cybersecurity.

Securing critical infrastructure, such as power grids, healthcare systems, and transportation networks, is essential to prevent devastating cyber-attacks that could have far-reaching consequences.

Supply chain security is another area of concern, as attackers may exploit vulnerabilities in the supply chain to compromise organizations.

Evaluating and mitigating these risks should be part of an organization's cybersecurity strategy.

Resilience and incident response planning are critical components of preparing for future cybersecurity challenges.

Organizations must have plans in place to quickly respond to security incidents, contain threats, and recover from cyberattacks.

Regularly testing these plans through tabletop exercises and simulations helps ensure they are effective when needed.

Technological advancements, such as quantum computing, present both opportunities and challenges in the field of cybersecurity.

Quantum computing has the potential to break current encryption methods, making it essential for organizations to start exploring quantum-resistant encryption techniques.

Preparing for future cybersecurity challenges also requires organizations to adopt a risk-based approach to security. Identifying and prioritizing assets and data that are most critical to the organization's operations is essential in allocating resources effectively.

The evolving threat landscape makes threat hunting an important part of cybersecurity preparation. Proactive threat hunting involves actively searching for signs of malicious activity within an organization's network and systems.

Threat hunting teams use advanced analytics and threat intelligence to identify potential threats before they escalate.

In summary, preparing for future cybersecurity challenges is an ongoing process that requires vigilance, adaptability, and collaboration.

As technology continues to advance, so do the tactics and techniques of cybercriminals.

To stay ahead of emerging threats, organizations and individuals must invest in cybersecurity education, adopt advanced technologies, and foster a culture of security awareness.

By recognizing the evolving nature of cyber threats and taking proactive steps to mitigate risks, we can better protect our digital assets and secure the future of our interconnected world.

BOOK 3
CYBERWATCH CHRONICLES
FROM NOVICE TO NINJA IN CYBER DEFENSE
ROB BOTWRIGHT

Chapter 1: The Novice's Path to Cybersecurity

Embracing a career in cybersecurity can be a rewarding and fulfilling journey in today's digital age, where the importance of securing information and technology has never been greater.

Cybersecurity professionals play a critical role in safeguarding organizations, individuals, and society from the ever-present and evolving threat landscape.

As the world becomes increasingly reliant on technology, the demand for cybersecurity experts continues to grow, offering a plethora of career opportunities and pathways.

Choosing a career in cybersecurity often begins with a passion for technology, a fascination with cybersecurity challenges, and a desire to make a positive impact on the digital world.

Cybersecurity is a multidisciplinary field that encompasses various domains, including network security, application security, incident response, penetration testing, and security analysis.

This diversity allows individuals to explore and specialize in areas that align with their interests and expertise.

A career in cybersecurity offers the chance to work in diverse industries, such as finance, healthcare, government, and technology, as virtually every sector requires robust cybersecurity measures to protect sensitive data and systems.

One of the most appealing aspects of a cybersecurity career is the constant learning and intellectual stimulation it provides.

Cybersecurity is a dynamic field where new threats and vulnerabilities emerge regularly, necessitating continuous education and skill development.

Cybersecurity professionals must stay informed about the latest attack techniques, security tools, and best practices to remain effective in their roles.

Furthermore, the cybersecurity community is known for its collaborative and supportive nature, with professionals often sharing knowledge, insights, and experiences to help one another.

This sense of camaraderie fosters growth and helps individuals overcome challenges they may encounter during their careers.

A career in cybersecurity can be financially rewarding, with competitive salaries and job security due to the high demand for skilled professionals.

Organizations are willing to invest in cybersecurity to protect their assets and reputation, making cybersecurity roles well-compensated.

Cybersecurity professionals also have the opportunity to work remotely, which provides flexibility and work-life balance, a significant advantage in today's job market.

The educational pathways to a career in cybersecurity are diverse, making it accessible to individuals with varying backgrounds and levels of experience.

While some cybersecurity roles require a bachelor's degree in computer science or a related field, others value practical experience and certifications.

Certifications, such as Certified Information Systems Security Professional (CISSP), Certified Ethical Hacker (CEH), and Certified Information Security Manager (CISM), can enhance one's qualifications and career prospects.

Many educational institutions and online platforms offer cybersecurity courses and training programs, making it possible for individuals to acquire the necessary skills and knowledge.

A career in cybersecurity offers numerous career advancement opportunities, allowing individuals to progress from entry-level positions to more senior roles.

These career paths often include positions such as security analyst, security engineer, security architect, and chief information security officer (CISO).

Cybersecurity professionals can also transition into specialized areas, such as cloud security, incident response, or threat hunting, based on their interests and expertise.

The demand for cybersecurity professionals is expected to continue growing in the coming years as technology becomes even more integral to our daily lives.

This growth means that individuals entering the field can look forward to a stable and promising career with many opportunities for growth and specialization.

Ethical hacking, also known as penetration testing, is a fascinating and well-compensated career within cybersecurity.

Ethical hackers use their skills to identify vulnerabilities in systems and applications, helping organizations patch weaknesses before malicious hackers can exploit them.

This role allows individuals to think like hackers while working to protect systems and data.

Cybersecurity consulting firms, government agencies, and major corporations often employ ethical hackers to assess their security posture.

Incident response professionals are crucial to minimizing the impact of cybersecurity incidents.

These experts are responsible for detecting, analyzing, and mitigating security breaches and helping organizations recover from cyberattacks.

Incident response professionals must be highly organized, calm under pressure, and capable of making critical decisions to address security incidents effectively.

Security architects design and implement security measures to protect an organization's systems, networks, and data.

They create security plans, select appropriate technologies, and ensure that security controls are integrated into the organization's infrastructure.

Security architects need a deep understanding of cybersecurity principles and a holistic view of an organization's security needs.

Security analysts play a vital role in monitoring an organization's network for security threats.

They analyze logs, alerts, and network traffic to detect suspicious activity and respond to potential threats promptly.

Security analysts often work in security operations centers (SOCs) and collaborate with incident response teams to address security incidents.

Chief information security officers (CISOs) are senior executives responsible for an organization's overall cybersecurity strategy and management.

CISOs oversee cybersecurity policies, compliance, and risk management, making critical decisions to protect the organization from cyber threats.

To become a CISO, individuals typically need extensive experience in cybersecurity and strong leadership skills.

The future of cybersecurity promises exciting developments, as emerging technologies like artificial intelligence and quantum computing present new challenges and opportunities.

AI-powered security tools can enhance threat detection and response, automating tasks and identifying anomalies in real-time.

Quantum computing, on the other hand, may require the development of quantum-resistant encryption to protect data in the post-quantum era.

The convergence of cybersecurity and privacy is another area of growth, with increased focus on data protection regulations like GDPR and CCPA.

As data privacy becomes a paramount concern, cybersecurity professionals with expertise in privacy regulations will be in high demand.

In summary, embracing a career in cybersecurity offers a multitude of benefits, from intellectual stimulation and financial rewards to job security and the opportunity to make a positive impact on society.

The field's diversity, continuous learning, and supportive community make it an attractive choice for individuals interested in technology and security.

With the growing demand for cybersecurity professionals and the ever-evolving threat landscape, now is an excellent time to embark on a cybersecurity career journey. Novice cybersecurity professionals embarking on their careers must develop a foundational set of essential skills to succeed in this dynamic and critical field. These skills serve as the building blocks upon which more advanced knowledge and expertise are constructed.

First and foremost, novice cybersecurity professionals must acquire a deep understanding of computer networks and their components.

A solid grasp of network protocols, topologies, and architecture is crucial because networks serve as the backbone of digital communication and data exchange.

Novices should familiarize themselves with concepts like IP addressing, subnetting, routing, and switching, as they are fundamental to network security.

Moreover, gaining proficiency in network troubleshooting and packet analysis tools is invaluable for identifying and mitigating security incidents.

In addition to network knowledge, novices must develop a strong foundation in operating systems.

Understanding how various operating systems work, including Windows, Linux, and macOS, is essential because these systems underpin nearly all computing devices.

Proficiency in administering and securing these operating systems is vital to protect against vulnerabilities and threats.

Furthermore, learning the basics of system administration, including user management, permissions, and file systems, is crucial for maintaining secure computing environments.

Comprehensive knowledge of cybersecurity fundamentals is another essential skill for novice professionals.

This includes understanding the principles of confidentiality, integrity, and availability (CIA), which form the core of information security.

Familiarity with the CIA triad helps novices identify security objectives and make informed decisions about implementing security controls.

Novices should also learn about the different types of threats and attack vectors, such as malware, social engineering, and unauthorized access.

Knowing how these threats work is crucial for developing effective security measures.

One of the key skills novice cybersecurity professionals must cultivate is the ability to assess and manage risk.

Risk assessment involves evaluating the likelihood and potential impact of security incidents and vulnerabilities.

This skill helps professionals prioritize security efforts and allocate resources effectively.

Moreover, novice professionals should learn how to create and implement security policies, procedures, and guidelines.

These documents serve as a roadmap for securing an organization's assets and defining acceptable behavior.

Creating clear and enforceable policies is essential for maintaining a secure environment and ensuring compliance with relevant regulations.

Another critical skill for novice cybersecurity professionals is vulnerability assessment and management.

This involves identifying and prioritizing vulnerabilities within an organization's systems, applications, and infrastructure.

Professionals should be able to use vulnerability scanning tools to discover weaknesses and recommend remediation strategies.

Novices should also become proficient in the use of security tools and technologies commonly employed in the field.

This includes firewalls, intrusion detection and prevention systems (IDPS), antivirus software, and encryption solutions.

Understanding how to configure and operate these tools is vital for safeguarding against various threats.

Furthermore, novices should gain knowledge of cybersecurity best practices and industry standards.

Familiarity with frameworks like the National Institute of Standards and Technology (NIST) Cybersecurity Framework and ISO 27001 can guide security efforts and compliance.

Additionally, novices should keep abreast of emerging threats and trends by staying informed through industry publications, conferences, and online forums.

An essential skill for novice cybersecurity professionals is incident detection and response.

Being able to identify security incidents and respond swiftly is critical for minimizing damage and restoring normal operations.

This skill involves monitoring network traffic, analyzing logs, and employing incident response plans.

Moreover, novices must develop strong analytical and problem-solving abilities.

Cybersecurity often involves complex and rapidly evolving threats, which require professionals to investigate and resolve security incidents effectively.

The ability to think critically, analyze data, and make informed decisions is invaluable in this regard.

Furthermore, novices should hone their communication skills.

Cybersecurity professionals must communicate clearly and effectively with colleagues, management, and external stakeholders.

This includes documenting security incidents, providing security awareness training, and conveying security risks to non-technical personnel.

Collaboration is a key aspect of cybersecurity, and professionals must work together to address security challenges effectively.

Understanding the importance of teamwork and being able to collaborate with colleagues from various departments is crucial for achieving security goals.

Another critical skill for novice cybersecurity professionals is knowledge of compliance and regulatory requirements.

Many industries have specific regulations governing the protection of sensitive data, such as healthcare (HIPAA), finance (GLBA), and data privacy (GDPR).

Novices should understand these regulations and their implications for security practices.

Furthermore, novices should develop an ethical mindset and a strong sense of integrity.

Cybersecurity professionals often have access to sensitive information and systems, and trust is paramount.

Maintaining ethical behavior and adhering to a code of conduct are essential for building trust and credibility in the field.

Lastly, novice cybersecurity professionals must cultivate a commitment to continuous learning and improvement.

The field of cybersecurity is constantly evolving, with new threats and technologies emerging regularly.

Staying up-to-date with industry developments and pursuing further education and certifications is essential for career growth and maintaining expertise.

In summary, novice cybersecurity professionals embarking on their careers should focus on developing a foundational set of essential skills.

These skills encompass network and operating system knowledge, cybersecurity fundamentals, risk assessment, policy creation, vulnerability management, and proficiency in security tools and technologies.

Additionally, professionals should emphasize incident detection and response, analytical and problem-solving abilities, effective communication, collaboration, compliance knowledge, ethical behavior, and a commitment to lifelong learning.

By mastering these essential skills, novice cybersecurity professionals can build a solid foundation for a successful and rewarding career in the field.

Chapter 2: Building a Strong Cyber Defense Foundation

Foundational concepts of cybersecurity form the bedrock upon which the entire field is built, providing essential principles and knowledge for safeguarding digital assets and data.

These concepts are essential for individuals and organizations seeking to protect themselves in an increasingly interconnected and digitized world.

One of the core principles of cybersecurity is confidentiality, which means ensuring that sensitive information remains private and is only accessible to authorized parties.

Confidentiality is vital because it prevents unauthorized access or disclosure of sensitive data, such as personal information, financial records, and trade secrets.

To achieve confidentiality, cybersecurity measures like encryption, access controls, and secure data storage are implemented.

Another foundational concept is integrity, which focuses on the accuracy and trustworthiness of data and information.

Integrity ensures that data remains unaltered and reliable throughout its lifecycle, guarding against unauthorized changes or tampering.

Methods for maintaining data integrity include checksums, digital signatures, and data validation processes.

Availability is a critical aspect of cybersecurity, emphasizing the need for systems and data to be accessible and functional when required.

Ensuring availability involves protecting against disruptions, such as denial-of-service attacks or hardware failures, to maintain uninterrupted access to resources.

Cybersecurity strategies for availability include redundancy, load balancing, and disaster recovery planning.

Authentication is a fundamental concept in cybersecurity, verifying the identity of users or systems before granting access to resources.

Authentication methods include passwords, biometrics, smart cards, and multi-factor authentication (MFA), which combine multiple authentication factors for enhanced security.

Authorization complements authentication by determining what actions or resources users or systems are allowed to access based on their authenticated identity.

Authorization mechanisms are crucial for enforcing the principle of least privilege, limiting access rights to the minimum necessary for a user's role.

Accountability and auditing are essential concepts for tracking and monitoring activities within a system or network.

Accountability ensures that actions are attributed to specific users or entities, making it possible to trace activities back to responsible parties.

Auditing involves recording and reviewing system events, logs, and access records to detect anomalies and maintain a historical record of activities.

Risk management is a foundational concept that involves identifying, assessing, and mitigating potential cybersecurity risks.

Risk assessment helps organizations prioritize security efforts and allocate resources effectively to protect against threats and vulnerabilities.

Cybersecurity professionals often use risk assessment frameworks and methodologies to guide their risk management practices.

Defense in depth is a core strategy in cybersecurity that involves employing multiple layers of security controls to protect against a variety of threats.

This approach recognizes that no single security measure is foolproof, and a layered defense increases the overall security posture.

Layers may include firewalls, intrusion detection systems, antivirus software, and security awareness training for users.

Threat modeling is a process used to identify potential threats and vulnerabilities within a system or application.

By analyzing potential attack vectors and weaknesses, organizations can proactively address security flaws and design more robust systems.

Threat modeling is an integral part of secure software development and system design.

Security policies and procedures provide guidelines and standards for organizations to follow in maintaining cybersecurity.

These policies define acceptable behaviors, responsibilities, and expectations related to security practices.

Effective security policies and procedures are crucial for ensuring consistency and adherence to security best practices.

Incident response is a foundational concept for dealing with security breaches and cyberattacks effectively.

Having a well-defined incident response plan in place enables organizations to respond promptly to security incidents, minimize damage, and facilitate recovery.

Incident response plans typically include roles and responsibilities, communication protocols, and escalation procedures.

Security awareness and training are fundamental for educating individuals within an organization about cybersecurity best practices.

Well-informed and vigilant users are essential for preventing security incidents caused by human error or social engineering attacks.

Regular training programs help individuals recognize and respond to potential threats.

Cryptography is a foundational technology in cybersecurity that enables secure communication and data protection.

Cryptography techniques, such as encryption and decryption, help safeguard sensitive information from unauthorized access or interception.

Cryptographic algorithms and key management are essential components of cryptographic systems.

Security assessment and testing involve evaluating the security of systems, applications, and networks to identify vulnerabilities and weaknesses.

Methods like penetration testing, vulnerability scanning, and security code reviews help organizations discover and address security flaws.

Security assessment and testing are essential for maintaining a robust security posture.

Security architecture and design play a pivotal role in cybersecurity by defining the structure and layout of secure systems and networks.

Well-designed security architecture incorporates security controls, best practices, and risk management principles into the overall system design.

Secure coding practices are crucial for developing software and applications that are resilient to security threats.

Security-focused coding guidelines and techniques help developers write code that is less susceptible to vulnerabilities and exploits.

Secure coding practices are integral to preventing software vulnerabilities.

Security incident management is a critical concept in handling and responding to security incidents effectively.

This process involves identifying, reporting, and managing security incidents to minimize their impact and prevent recurrence.

Security incident management often includes incident detection, analysis, containment, eradication, and recovery.

Security monitoring and surveillance involve continuously monitoring systems, networks, and logs to detect and respond to security threats.

Automated monitoring tools and security information and event management (SIEM) systems help organizations identify suspicious activities and potential breaches in real-time.

Security professionals analyze the data collected through monitoring to make informed decisions about incident response.

Security culture and awareness within an organization are foundational concepts that emphasize the importance of fostering a security-conscious mindset among all employees.

A strong security culture encourages individuals to take responsibility for cybersecurity and promotes a collective effort to protect digital assets.

Security governance refers to the processes, policies, and structures that guide an organization's approach to cybersecurity.

Effective security governance ensures that cybersecurity aligns with an organization's business objectives and regulatory requirements.

It also defines roles and responsibilities for managing and overseeing security efforts.

In summary, foundational concepts of cybersecurity form the basis for understanding and implementing effective security measures and practices.

These concepts encompass principles like confidentiality, integrity, and availability, as well as essential practices like authentication, authorization, and risk management.

By embracing these foundational concepts, individuals and organizations can build a strong and resilient cybersecurity framework to protect against a wide range of threats and vulnerabilities.

Establishing core security practices is essential for individuals and organizations alike, as the digital landscape becomes increasingly complex and interconnected.

These practices serve as the foundation for creating a secure environment and protecting sensitive information from a wide range of threats.

One of the fundamental security practices is to regularly update and patch all software and operating systems to address known vulnerabilities.

Unpatched systems can be exploited by cybercriminals, so staying up-to-date with security updates is critical.

Moreover, employing strong access controls is crucial for managing who has access to various systems and data.

Implementing user authentication, authorization, and strong password policies helps ensure that only authorized personnel can access sensitive information.

Encryption is a core security practice that involves encoding data to protect it from unauthorized access.

Using encryption for data at rest and in transit helps safeguard information even if it falls into the wrong hands.

Another critical practice is to regularly back up data to ensure its availability in case of hardware failures, data corruption, or cyberattacks.

Data backups should be performed regularly and stored securely to prevent data loss.

Network security practices involve configuring firewalls, intrusion detection systems, and intrusion prevention systems to monitor and filter incoming and outgoing network traffic.

These security measures help protect the network from unauthorized access and cyber threats.

Security awareness and training programs are vital for educating individuals within an organization about potential security risks and best practices.

Regular training helps employees recognize and respond to security threats effectively.

Implementing strong endpoint security solutions, such as antivirus software and host-based firewalls, is essential for protecting individual devices like computers and smartphones from malware and cyberattacks.

Regularly auditing and monitoring system logs and network traffic helps detect and respond to security incidents promptly.

Incident response plans and procedures should be in place to guide actions and communication during and after a security incident.

Having a well-documented incident response plan can minimize the impact of security breaches.

Security governance practices establish the framework and processes for managing security efforts within an organization.

These practices include defining roles and responsibilities, creating security policies and procedures, and ensuring compliance with relevant regulations.

Performing risk assessments is crucial for identifying and prioritizing potential security risks and vulnerabilities.

Risk assessment helps organizations allocate resources effectively to address the most critical security concerns.

Secure software development practices involve implementing security measures throughout the software development lifecycle to prevent vulnerabilities and exploits.

By building security into the development process, organizations can reduce the likelihood of software-related security issues.

Physical security practices are essential for safeguarding physical assets, such as servers and data centers, from unauthorized access.

Access controls, surveillance, and secure facilities help protect physical infrastructure.

Implementing a secure supply chain process ensures that hardware and software components from third-party vendors meet security standards and do not introduce vulnerabilities.

Vulnerability management practices involve regularly scanning and assessing systems and applications for vulnerabilities and addressing them promptly.

Timely vulnerability remediation is critical for reducing the risk of exploitation.

Security testing and assessment practices, such as penetration testing and security code reviews, help identify security weaknesses in systems, applications, and networks.

These practices enable organizations to proactively address vulnerabilities before they can be exploited.

Implementing a comprehensive incident response plan is crucial for effectively managing and mitigating security incidents.

The plan should include procedures for incident detection, containment, eradication, and recovery.

Creating a security incident response team with well-defined roles and responsibilities is essential for executing the incident response plan effectively.

Security awareness and training programs help educate employees about security risks and best practices.

These programs should cover topics such as phishing awareness, password security, and safe web browsing.

Establishing a secure remote work policy is essential in today's digital workplace, as many employees work remotely or use mobile devices to access company resources.

The policy should include guidelines for secure remote access, device security, and data protection.

Secure data disposal practices involve properly disposing of sensitive information and hardware to prevent data breaches.

Shredding paper documents and securely wiping data from storage devices are essential steps in data disposal.

Security incident documentation is crucial for maintaining a record of security incidents, their impact, and the response actions taken.

Detailed documentation is valuable for post-incident analysis and reporting.

Implementing security best practices for software development includes conducting security reviews, code audits, and threat modeling to identify and address vulnerabilities in applications.

Secure coding practices help prevent common security flaws in software.

Security awareness and training programs should include ongoing education and reinforcement of security best practices to keep employees informed and vigilant.

Regularly reviewing and updating security policies and procedures ensures that they remain current and aligned with evolving security threats and technologies.

Security governance practices establish the framework and processes for managing security efforts within an organization.

Security policies and procedures define acceptable security behavior and provide guidelines for compliance.

Vulnerability management practices involve identifying, prioritizing, and mitigating vulnerabilities in systems and applications to reduce the risk of exploitation.

Security incident response planning and testing help organizations prepare for and respond to security incidents effectively.

Implementing multi-factor authentication (MFA) adds an additional layer of security by requiring users to provide multiple forms of verification before gaining access to systems or data.

Regularly testing and assessing the security of systems and networks help identify vulnerabilities and weaknesses that need to be addressed.

Security assessments, such as penetration testing and vulnerability scanning, help organizations proactively identify and remediate security issues.

Security monitoring and surveillance practices involve continuously monitoring systems, networks, and logs to detect and respond to security threats in real-time.

Incident response planning and testing ensure that organizations are prepared to respond effectively to security incidents.

Implementing security controls and measures, such as firewalls, intrusion detection systems, and access controls, helps protect systems and data from unauthorized access and cyber threats.

Physical security practices, such as access controls and surveillance, help protect physical assets from unauthorized access and theft.

Security awareness and training programs educate employees about security risks and best practices, empowering them to recognize and respond to potential threats.

Secure software development practices help prevent vulnerabilities and security flaws in software applications by incorporating security into the development process.

Security governance practices provide the framework and processes for managing security efforts within an organization.

In summary, establishing core security practices is essential for individuals and organizations to protect against a wide range of security threats and vulnerabilities.

These practices encompass areas such as software updates, access controls, encryption, backup, network security, and security awareness.

By implementing these foundational security measures and continuously assessing and adapting to evolving threats, organizations can enhance their overall security posture and reduce the risk of security incidents.

Chapter 3: Understanding Common Cyber Threats

Identifying and classifying cyber threats is a critical aspect of cybersecurity, as it enables individuals and organizations to understand the nature of potential risks they may face in the digital landscape.

Cyber threats come in various forms, each with its own characteristics, motivations, and methods.

To effectively protect against these threats, it is essential to have a comprehensive understanding of the types of threats that exist and how to classify them.

One common classification of cyber threats distinguishes between external and internal threats.

External threats originate from outside an organization's network and can include attacks by hackers, cybercriminals, or state-sponsored entities.

These threats often target vulnerabilities in network infrastructure, software, or individuals.

In contrast, internal threats emanate from within an organization and can involve employees, contractors, or other insiders who may intentionally or unintentionally compromise security.

Examples of internal threats include data breaches caused by employees mishandling sensitive information or insider attacks aimed at stealing data.

Another way to classify cyber threats is based on their primary objectives, which can be broadly categorized as data breaches, financial gain, disruption of services, and espionage.

Data breaches involve the unauthorized access, theft, or exposure of sensitive information, such as customer data or intellectual property.

Financial gain-driven threats include various forms of cybercrime, such as ransomware attacks, phishing schemes, and credit card fraud, where attackers aim to profit financially from their activities.

Threats seeking to disrupt services can lead to downtime, loss of productivity, and reputational damage for organizations.

These threats can encompass distributed denial of service (DDoS) attacks or targeted efforts to disrupt critical infrastructure.

Espionage-related threats involve the theft of sensitive information for political, economic, or military purposes.

These threats are often associated with nation-states or advanced persistent threat (APT) groups seeking to gather intelligence or gain a competitive advantage.

Another classification of cyber threats considers the methods and techniques employed by threat actors.

Malware, a broad category of malicious software, includes viruses, worms, Trojans, and ransomware, among others.

These programs are designed to infiltrate systems, infect files, and execute harmful actions.

Phishing attacks involve fraudulent emails or messages designed to deceive recipients into revealing sensitive information, such as login credentials or financial data.

Social engineering tactics exploit human psychology and behavior to manipulate individuals into divulging confidential information or taking specific actions.

These tactics can include pretexting, baiting, or tailgating, where attackers exploit trust or authority.

Exploiting software vulnerabilities is a common tactic, with threat actors searching for weaknesses in software, applications, or systems that can be exploited to gain unauthorized access or control.

Zero-day vulnerabilities, in particular, are highly sought after because they are unpatched and offer a window of opportunity for attackers.

Advanced persistent threats (APTs) are characterized by targeted, long-term campaigns by highly skilled threat actors, often with nation-state backing, to infiltrate and exfiltrate data from specific organizations or industries.

Insider threats involve individuals within an organization who misuse their access privileges to compromise security, intentionally or unintentionally.

These individuals may have legitimate access to sensitive information, making them particularly dangerous.

Organized cybercrime groups operate as criminal organizations with the primary goal of making a profit through various cybercriminal activities, such as identity theft, fraud, and cyber extortion.

Cyber espionage involves state-sponsored actors or cybercriminals seeking to steal sensitive information from governments, organizations, or individuals for political, economic, or military purposes.

Hacktivism is driven by ideological or political motives, with hackers aiming to raise awareness or promote a specific cause through cyberattacks or website defacement.

Understanding and classifying cyber threats is essential for developing effective security strategies and countermeasures.

Threat intelligence, which involves collecting and analyzing information about potential threats, can provide valuable insights into the evolving threat landscape.

Threat intelligence feeds and services provide organizations with up-to-date information on emerging threats, helping them stay ahead of cyber adversaries.

Intrusion detection and prevention systems (IDPS) are critical tools for identifying and mitigating threats in real-time by monitoring network traffic and system activities for suspicious behavior.

Security information and event management (SIEM) solutions aggregate and correlate data from various sources to provide a holistic view of an organization's security posture and facilitate threat detection.

Firewalls and network security appliances help filter incoming and outgoing traffic to prevent unauthorized access and protect against known threats.

Antivirus software and endpoint protection solutions are essential for detecting and mitigating malware threats on individual devices.

Security awareness and training programs educate employees about the risks associated with cyber threats and empower them to recognize and respond to potential threats effectively.

Regular security assessments, including vulnerability scanning and penetration testing, help organizations identify and address weaknesses in their security defenses.

Cyber threat modeling is a proactive approach that involves identifying potential threats and vulnerabilities within a system or application to design robust security measures.

Incident response plans and procedures guide organizations in responding to and mitigating security incidents effectively.

Collaboration and information sharing within the cybersecurity community are essential for staying informed about emerging threats and best practices.

Understanding the motives, methods, and classifications of cyber threats is an ongoing process, as the threat landscape constantly evolves.

As new technologies emerge and threat actors adapt their tactics, organizations must remain vigilant and continuously update their cybersecurity strategies to stay one step ahead of cyber adversaries.

In summary, identifying and classifying cyber threats is a fundamental aspect of cybersecurity that enables organizations to protect their digital assets and sensitive information.

These threats can be categorized based on their objectives, methods, and origins, and understanding their nature is crucial for developing effective security measures.

By staying informed about emerging threats, leveraging threat intelligence, and implementing robust security practices and technologies, organizations can strengthen their defenses and mitigate the risks posed by cyber adversaries.

In the world of cybersecurity, real-world examples of common threats provide valuable insights into the types of risks that individuals and organizations face in the digital age.
One prevalent threat that people encounter daily is phishing, where malicious actors send deceptive emails or messages to trick recipients into revealing sensitive information.
For instance, a common phishing scenario might involve an email that appears to come from a trusted bank, asking the recipient to click on a link and provide their login credentials, ultimately leading to a compromised bank account.
Ransomware attacks represent another significant threat, where cybercriminals encrypt a victim's data and demand a ransom for its decryption.
An example is the WannaCry ransomware attack in 2017, which affected thousands of computers worldwide and disrupted critical services, illustrating the potentially devastating consequences of such attacks.
Malware, a broad category of malicious software, includes viruses, worms, and Trojans, which can infect computers and compromise data.
The infamous Stuxnet worm, discovered in 2010, is an example of sophisticated malware that targeted industrial systems, causing physical damage to Iran's nuclear facilities.
Distributed Denial of Service (DDoS) attacks aim to overwhelm a target's network or website with a flood of traffic, rendering it inaccessible.
The 2016 Dyn cyberattack disrupted internet services for users across the United States and Europe, underscoring the disruptive potential of DDoS attacks.
Identity theft is a prevalent threat in which cybercriminals steal personal information to commit fraud or gain unauthorized access to accounts.

In 2017, Equifax suffered a massive data breach, exposing the personal information of millions of individuals, highlighting the risks associated with identity theft.

Another common threat is the exploitation of software vulnerabilities, such as zero-day vulnerabilities that attackers leverage before developers can release patches.

The NotPetya ransomware, which spread globally in 2017, utilized a zero-day vulnerability in Windows to infect and disrupt numerous organizations.

Social engineering attacks rely on manipulating human psychology to deceive individuals into divulging sensitive information.

A classic example is pretexting, where an attacker poses as a trusted authority, such as a company executive, to trick an employee into disclosing confidential data.

Insider threats represent risks from within an organization, as employees or insiders may intentionally or unintentionally compromise security.

In 2013, Edward Snowden, a contractor for the National Security Agency (NSA), leaked classified documents, highlighting the potential consequences of insider threats.

Internet of Things (IoT) devices, while offering convenience, also introduce security vulnerabilities.

The Mirai botnet, discovered in 2016, exploited poorly secured IoT devices to launch large-scale DDoS attacks, demonstrating the risks associated with insecure IoT deployments.

Supply chain attacks involve compromising the security of a trusted vendor or supplier to gain access to a target organization's systems.

In 2020, the SolarWinds cyberattack exploited a compromised software update to breach numerous government and corporate networks, illustrating the reach of supply chain attacks.

Data breaches continue to be a pervasive threat, with cybercriminals targeting organizations to steal sensitive data.

The 2013 Target data breach exposed credit card information for millions of customers, resulting in financial losses and reputational damage for the retailer.

Rogue software or malicious apps pose a risk to users who unwittingly download and install them.

For example, in 2017, the Android malware Judy infected millions of devices through malicious apps on the Google Play Store.

Business email compromise (BEC) attacks involve impersonating executives or vendors to trick employees into making fraudulent transactions.

In 2019, the FBI reported billions of dollars in losses due to BEC scams, emphasizing the financial impact of such attacks.

Advanced Persistent Threats (APTs) are sophisticated, long-term cyber campaigns typically associated with nation-state actors.

APT29, also known as Cozy Bear, is an example of a state-sponsored group that has conducted cyber espionage activities globally.

Pharming attacks manipulate DNS settings or domain names to redirect users to malicious websites, potentially compromising their data.

In 2008, the DNSChanger malware infected millions of computers, redirecting users to fraudulent websites and affecting internet browsing.

Cryptojacking involves using a victim's computer or device to mine cryptocurrency without their consent or knowledge.

This covert practice can slow down devices and drain their resources, impacting user experience.

In 2017, the Coinhive cryptojacking script gained notoriety for exploiting websites to mine cryptocurrency using visitors' CPUs.

Fake antivirus software scams prey on users' fears of malware infections by offering bogus security products.

One example is the "MS Antivirus" scam, which tricked users into purchasing fake antivirus software.

Brute force attacks involve repeatedly trying various combinations of passwords until the correct one is found.

Such attacks can be time-consuming but may succeed if users have weak or easily guessable passwords.

The widespread use of the internet and digital technologies has created an environment where cyber threats are constant and evolving.

These real-world examples of common threats illustrate the diverse tactics and motivations of cybercriminals and underscore the importance of robust cybersecurity measures to mitigate risks and protect sensitive information and digital assets.

Chapter 4: Mastering Network Security

Network security is a critical component of modern cybersecurity strategies, encompassing a wide range of measures and practices designed to protect the confidentiality, integrity, and availability of data transmitted over networks.

The increasing reliance on digital communication and the proliferation of network-connected devices have made network security more vital than ever before.

Effective network security helps organizations safeguard sensitive information, maintain the trust of their customers, and prevent data breaches and cyberattacks.

Network security involves the implementation of various technologies, policies, and procedures to secure the underlying infrastructure of computer networks.

Firewalls are essential network security devices that filter and monitor incoming and outgoing network traffic based on a set of predefined rules and security policies.

They act as a barrier between an organization's internal network and the external internet, helping to prevent unauthorized access and protect against known threats.

Intrusion Detection Systems (IDS) and Intrusion Prevention Systems (IPS) are network security tools that monitor network traffic for suspicious activities or patterns that may indicate a security breach.

IDS passively detect potential threats, while IPS can actively block or mitigate threats in real-time.

Virtual Private Networks (VPNs) provide secure and encrypted communication channels over public networks, such as the internet, allowing remote users to access an organization's network securely.

VPNs are crucial for ensuring the privacy and security of data transmitted between remote locations.

Secure Sockets Layer (SSL) and Transport Layer Security (TLS) protocols are cryptographic protocols that provide secure communication over the internet.

They encrypt data exchanged between a user's web browser and a website's server, ensuring that sensitive information, such as login credentials and financial data, remains confidential.

Access Control Lists (ACLs) are used to restrict and control network traffic based on predefined rules and policies.

They are typically implemented on routers and switches to regulate the flow of data within a network.

Network segmentation is a network security strategy that involves dividing a network into smaller, isolated segments to contain potential security breaches and limit lateral movement by attackers.

Each network segment can have its own security measures and access controls.

Intrusion Detection Systems (IDS) and Intrusion Prevention Systems (IPS) are network security tools that monitor network traffic for suspicious activities or patterns that may indicate a security breach.

IDS passively detect potential threats, while IPS can actively block or mitigate threats in real-time.

Virtual Private Networks (VPNs) provide secure and encrypted communication channels over public networks, such as the internet, allowing remote users to access an organization's network securely.

VPNs are crucial for ensuring the privacy and security of data transmitted between remote locations.

Secure Sockets Layer (SSL) and Transport Layer Security (TLS) protocols are cryptographic protocols that provide secure communication over the internet.

They encrypt data exchanged between a user's web browser and a website's server, ensuring that sensitive information, such as login credentials and financial data, remains confidential.

Access Control Lists (ACLs) are used to restrict and control network traffic based on predefined rules and policies.

They are typically implemented on routers and switches to regulate the flow of data within a network.

Network segmentation is a network security strategy that involves dividing a network into smaller, isolated segments to contain potential security breaches and limit lateral movement by attackers.

Each network segment can have its own security measures and access controls.

Intrusion Detection Systems (IDS) and Intrusion Prevention Systems (IPS) are network security tools that monitor network traffic for suspicious activities or patterns that may indicate a security breach.

IDS passively detect potential threats, while IPS can actively block or mitigate threats in real-time.

Virtual Private Networks (VPNs) provide secure and encrypted communication channels over public networks, such as the internet, allowing remote users to access an organization's network securely.

VPNs are crucial for ensuring the privacy and security of data transmitted between remote locations.

Secure Sockets Layer (SSL) and Transport Layer Security (TLS) protocols are cryptographic protocols that provide secure communication over the internet.

They encrypt data exchanged between a user's web browser and a website's server, ensuring that sensitive information, such as login credentials and financial data, remains confidential.

Access Control Lists (ACLs) are used to restrict and control network traffic based on predefined rules and policies.

They are typically implemented on routers and switches to regulate the flow of data within a network.

Network segmentation is a network security strategy that involves dividing a network into smaller, isolated segments to contain potential security breaches and limit lateral movement by attackers.

Each network segment can have its own security measures and access controls.

Intrusion Detection Systems (IDS) and Intrusion Prevention Systems (IPS) are network security tools that monitor network traffic for suspicious activities or patterns that may indicate a security breach.

IDS passively detect potential threats, while IPS can actively block or mitigate threats in real-time.

Virtual Private Networks (VPNs) provide secure and encrypted communication channels over public networks, such as the internet, allowing remote users to access an organization's network securely.

VPNs are crucial for ensuring the privacy and security of data transmitted between remote locations.

Secure Sockets Layer (SSL) and Transport Layer Security (TLS) protocols are cryptographic protocols that provide secure communication over the internet.

They encrypt data exchanged between a user's web browser and a website's server, ensuring that sensitive information, such as login credentials and financial data, remains confidential.

Access Control Lists (ACLs) are used to restrict and control network traffic based on predefined rules and policies.

They are typically implemented on routers and switches to regulate the flow of data within a network.

Network segmentation is a network security strategy that involves dividing a network into smaller, isolated segments to contain potential security breaches and limit lateral movement by attackers.

Each network segment can have its own security measures and access controls.

Firewalls play a crucial role in network security by inspecting and filtering incoming and outgoing traffic, blocking unauthorized access attempts, and preventing the spread of malware.

Firewalls can be hardware-based or software-based, and they are often configured to enforce security policies based on port numbers, protocols, and IP addresses.

Intrusion Detection Systems (IDS) are network security tools designed to monitor network traffic and identify suspicious or malicious activity.

Securing networks is a critical task in today's interconnected world, where the potential for cyber threats and attacks is ever-present.

Effective network security requires a combination of technologies, policies, and practices that work together to protect data and systems from unauthorized access and malicious activity.

One of the fundamental best practices for securing networks is to implement a strong firewall to act as a barrier between the internal network and the external world, filtering traffic and blocking known threats.

Firewalls can be hardware-based or software-based, and they should be configured to enforce strict security policies based on specific criteria, such as IP addresses, port numbers, and protocols.

In addition to a strong firewall, it's essential to regularly update and patch network devices and software to address known vulnerabilities and ensure that security features are up to date.

Vulnerability management programs can help organizations identify and prioritize these updates to minimize the risk of exploitation.

Access control is another crucial aspect of network security, involving the management of user accounts and permissions to ensure that only authorized individuals have access to network resources.

Implementing strong password policies, enforcing multi-factor authentication, and regularly reviewing and revoking access rights for former employees are all part of effective access control practices.

Network segmentation is a recommended strategy to enhance security by dividing a network into smaller, isolated segments, limiting the lateral movement of attackers in case of a breach.

Each network segment should have its own security measures and access controls, reducing the potential impact of a security incident.

Encryption is a powerful tool for protecting data in transit over a network, preventing unauthorized interception and eavesdropping.

Implementing protocols like SSL/TLS for web traffic and VPNs for remote access can ensure that data remains confidential and secure during transmission.

Regular network monitoring is vital for detecting and responding to security incidents promptly.

Intrusion Detection Systems (IDS) and Intrusion Prevention Systems (IPS) can help identify suspicious or malicious activities on the network, allowing for timely intervention and mitigation.

Continuous monitoring can also provide valuable insights into network traffic patterns and anomalies that may indicate a security breach.

Security information and event management (SIEM) solutions are valuable for aggregating and analyzing data from various network sources, helping organizations gain a holistic view of their security posture.

They can correlate data to identify potential threats and generate alerts for further investigation.

To further enhance network security, organizations should implement strong authentication mechanisms, such as multi-factor authentication (MFA), which requires users to provide multiple forms of verification before gaining access to network resources.

This additional layer of security can significantly reduce the risk of unauthorized access.

Regularly backing up critical data and systems is a fundamental practice for network security, ensuring that data can be recovered in case of a data breach or system failure.

Backups should be stored securely and tested regularly to ensure they are reliable.

Employee training and awareness programs are essential for creating a culture of security within an organization.

Educating employees about the risks of social engineering attacks, phishing scams, and other common threats can help them recognize and report potential security incidents.

Physical security measures should not be overlooked, as physical access to network infrastructure can lead to data breaches.

Securing server rooms, data centers, and network equipment with access controls and surveillance can prevent unauthorized individuals from tampering with network assets.

Regularly conducting security assessments, including vulnerability scanning and penetration testing, can help organizations identify and address weaknesses in their network defenses.

These assessments simulate real-world attack scenarios to evaluate the effectiveness of security measures and policies.

Incident response plans and procedures should be in place to guide organizations in responding to security incidents promptly and effectively.

Having a well-defined incident response team and communication plan is crucial for minimizing the impact of security breaches.

Regularly updating and testing these plans ensures that they remain relevant and effective.

Compliance with industry-specific regulations and standards is often required for organizations to demonstrate their commitment to network security.

Adhering to frameworks like the Payment Card Industry Data Security Standard (PCI DSS) or the Health Insurance Portability and Accountability Act (HIPAA) can help ensure the protection of sensitive data.

Network security should be an ongoing and evolving process, adapting to new threats and technologies.

Regular security awareness training for employees, threat intelligence sharing, and staying informed about emerging threats and vulnerabilities are all part of a proactive approach to network security.

Collaboration with cybersecurity experts, industry peers, and government agencies can provide valuable insights and best practices for enhancing network security.

In summary, securing networks is a complex and dynamic task that requires a multi-faceted approach encompassing technology, policies, and practices.

Implementing strong firewalls, access controls, encryption, and monitoring are essential components of network security.

Regular updates, employee training, and incident response planning are crucial for maintaining a robust security posture.

By following best practices and staying vigilant, organizations can minimize the risk of security breaches and protect their valuable data and assets from cyber threats.

Chapter 5: Advanced Endpoint Protection

Endpoint security solutions and strategies play a pivotal role in protecting an organization's network and data in today's digital landscape.

Endpoints, such as computers, laptops, smartphones, and tablets, are the gateways to an organization's network and are vulnerable to a wide range of threats.

Endpoint security focuses on safeguarding these devices from malware, unauthorized access, data breaches, and other security risks.

One of the core elements of an effective endpoint security strategy is antivirus and anti-malware software, which is designed to detect and remove malicious software from endpoints.

These solutions use signature-based detection, behavior analysis, and heuristic algorithms to identify and quarantine threats.

In addition to traditional antivirus software, organizations can employ advanced endpoint detection and response (EDR) solutions that offer real-time monitoring and response capabilities.

Endpoint security strategies should also include regular software patch management to ensure that operating systems and applications are up to date with the latest security patches.

Unpatched vulnerabilities can be exploited by attackers to gain access to endpoints and compromise the network.

Endpoint encryption is another critical component of endpoint security, ensuring that sensitive data stored on devices remains confidential even if the device is lost or stolen.

Full-disk encryption and file-level encryption are commonly used to protect data at rest.

Mobile Device Management (MDM) solutions are essential for securing smartphones and tablets used within an organization.

MDM allows IT administrators to enforce security policies, remotely wipe devices in case of loss or theft, and control access to corporate resources.

Endpoint security strategies should incorporate the use of strong authentication methods, such as multi-factor authentication (MFA) and biometrics, to verify the identity of users accessing endpoints and data.

MFA requires users to provide multiple forms of verification, enhancing security.

Behavioral analytics and user and entity behavior analytics (UEBA) are increasingly important tools in endpoint security.

These solutions analyze user behavior and device activity to detect anomalies that may indicate a security threat, such as unusual login patterns or data access.

Endpoint security solutions should include firewall and intrusion detection and prevention capabilities to protect endpoints from network-based attacks.

Firewalls can filter incoming and outgoing traffic, while intrusion prevention systems can actively block or mitigate threats in real-time.

Web filtering and content filtering tools are essential for preventing users from accessing malicious websites and inappropriate content that could compromise security.

Email security solutions, including anti-phishing and email filtering tools, are critical for protecting endpoints from email-based attacks such as phishing and malware-laden attachments.

Endpoint security strategies should include robust endpoint backup and recovery solutions to ensure that critical data can be restored in case of data loss or ransomware attacks.

Data loss prevention (DLP) solutions are designed to prevent the unauthorized transfer or sharing of sensitive data, helping organizations maintain compliance and protect intellectual property.

Endpoint security should extend to the Internet of Things (IoT) devices, which are increasingly connected to corporate networks.

IoT security solutions can help monitor and manage the security of these devices, preventing them from becoming entry points for attackers.

To strengthen endpoint security, organizations should implement a comprehensive incident response plan that outlines the steps to take in case of a security breach involving endpoints.

This plan should include communication protocols, forensic investigation procedures, and strategies for minimizing the impact of a breach.

Regular security awareness training for employees is vital in educating them about the risks associated with endpoint security and the importance of adhering to security policies.

Endpoint security solutions should integrate with a Security Information and Event Management (SIEM) system to provide centralized monitoring, analysis, and reporting of security events across the network.

This integration can help organizations identify and respond to threats more effectively.

Machine learning and artificial intelligence (AI) are increasingly being used in endpoint security solutions to detect and respond to advanced threats.

These technologies can analyze vast amounts of data to identify patterns and anomalies indicative of malicious activity.

Cloud-based endpoint security solutions offer scalability and flexibility, allowing organizations to protect remote and mobile users effectively.

They can also provide real-time threat intelligence and automatic updates to ensure that endpoints are always protected against the latest threats.

Endpoint security strategies should include regular vulnerability assessments and penetration testing to identify weaknesses in endpoint security measures.

These assessments help organizations proactively address security flaws before they can be exploited by attackers.

In summary, endpoint security solutions and strategies are essential for protecting an organization's network and data from a wide range of threats.

These solutions encompass antivirus and anti-malware software, encryption, mobile device management, strong authentication, behavioral analytics, and more.

By implementing a comprehensive endpoint security strategy, organizations can significantly reduce the risk of security breaches and ensure the integrity and confidentiality of their data and systems.

Protecting endpoints in today's evolving threat landscape is an increasingly challenging task for organizations of all sizes.

Endpoints, including laptops, desktops, smartphones, and tablets, are frequently targeted by cybercriminals due to their vulnerability and the potential access they provide to an organization's network and sensitive data.

The threat landscape continues to evolve with the emergence of new and sophisticated attack vectors, making it essential for organizations to adopt a proactive and multi-layered approach to endpoint security.

One of the key challenges in protecting endpoints is the rapid increase in the volume and complexity of malware and other malicious software.

Cybercriminals constantly develop new malware variants that can evade traditional signature-based antivirus solutions, making it crucial to complement these tools with advanced threat detection and prevention technologies.

Endpoint detection and response (EDR) solutions have gained prominence in recent years, providing organizations with real-time visibility into endpoint activities and the ability to detect and respond to advanced threats.

These solutions use behavioral analytics and machine learning to identify abnormal patterns of behavior that may indicate a security breach.

Phishing attacks, a common threat vector, have become more sophisticated, and cybercriminals use social engineering tactics to trick users into revealing sensitive information or clicking on malicious links.

Endpoint security strategies should include robust email security solutions to filter out phishing emails and malicious attachments, along with user training and awareness programs to educate employees about the dangers of phishing.

The rise of remote work and the use of personal devices for business purposes have expanded the attack surface for organizations, making it essential to secure endpoints wherever they are located.

Mobile device management (MDM) solutions help organizations manage and secure smartphones and tablets, enforce security policies, and remotely wipe devices in case of loss or theft.

Endpoint encryption is another critical component of endpoint security, ensuring that data on endpoints remains protected even if the device is compromised.

Full-disk encryption and file-level encryption are commonly used to safeguard sensitive information.

One significant threat that organizations face is the increasing prevalence of ransomware attacks.

Ransomware can encrypt an endpoint's data and demand a ransom for its release, causing significant disruptions and financial losses.

Endpoint security strategies should include regular data backups and recovery plans to ensure that critical data can be restored in case of a ransomware attack.

Implementing application whitelisting is another best practice for protecting endpoints.

Whitelisting allows organizations to specify which applications are allowed to run on endpoints, preventing unauthorized or malicious software from executing.

As organizations adopt cloud services and embrace hybrid work environments, it becomes crucial to extend endpoint security to cloud-based applications and services.

Cloud access security brokers (CASBs) can help organizations enforce security policies, monitor user activities, and protect data as it moves between endpoints and the cloud.

IoT devices, which are increasingly integrated into business environments, present additional security challenges.

These devices may lack built-in security features, making them vulnerable to exploitation.

Endpoint security strategies should include the monitoring and management of IoT devices to prevent them from becoming entry points for attackers.

Security information and event management (SIEM) solutions play a crucial role in endpoint security by providing centralized monitoring, analysis, and reporting of security events.

SIEM solutions can correlate data from multiple endpoints to detect and respond to threats effectively.

Endpoint security should extend beyond prevention to include incident response capabilities.

Organizations should have well-defined incident response plans in place, outlining the steps to take in case of a security breach involving endpoints.

Regularly testing these plans through tabletop exercises and simulations helps ensure that the response is efficient and effective.

Collaboration with external threat intelligence providers and information sharing within industry-specific groups can enhance an organization's ability to defend against evolving threats.

Machine learning and artificial intelligence (AI) are increasingly used in endpoint security to enhance threat detection and response.

These technologies can analyze vast amounts of data to identify patterns and anomalies indicative of malicious activity.

In summary, protecting endpoints in today's evolving threat landscape requires a multi-faceted approach that combines traditional antivirus solutions with advanced threat detection and response technologies.

Email security, encryption, mobile device management, and cloud security measures are all essential components of an effective endpoint security strategy.

Regular data backups, incident response planning, and collaboration with threat intelligence providers are crucial for mitigating the impact of security breaches.

Organizations must remain vigilant and adapt their endpoint security strategies to address emerging threats and protect their sensitive data and systems effectively.

Chapter 6: Security Monitoring and Incident Response

Monitoring tools and techniques are essential components of any modern organization's IT infrastructure, providing real-time visibility into the performance and security of systems, applications, and networks.

These tools play a critical role in ensuring the reliability, availability, and performance of IT resources, helping organizations identify and address issues proactively.

One of the primary objectives of monitoring tools is to provide continuous insight into the health and performance of an organization's IT environment.

These tools collect data from various sources, such as servers, network devices, and applications, and present it in a centralized dashboard or console.

Real-time monitoring tools offer the advantage of immediate alerts and notifications when anomalies or performance bottlenecks are detected.

Proactive monitoring can help IT teams respond quickly to issues, minimizing downtime and user disruption.

Performance monitoring tools are instrumental in tracking the performance of servers, applications, and infrastructure components.

These tools can measure key performance indicators (KPIs), such as response times, resource utilization, and transaction rates, allowing organizations to identify performance bottlenecks and optimize their IT environment.

Network monitoring tools are crucial for tracking the health and performance of an organization's network infrastructure.

They can monitor network traffic, bandwidth usage, and network device health, enabling IT teams to detect and troubleshoot network issues promptly.

Security monitoring tools are essential for identifying and mitigating security threats and vulnerabilities.

They can monitor network traffic for suspicious activities, scan for known vulnerabilities, and provide alerts for potential security breaches.

Log and event monitoring tools collect and analyze logs and events generated by various systems and applications.

These tools are vital for auditing and compliance purposes, as they can track user activities, system changes, and security incidents.

Application performance monitoring (APM) tools focus on the performance and availability of software applications.

APM tools can monitor application code execution, user interactions, and response times, helping organizations optimize their applications for better user experiences.

Cloud monitoring tools are designed to monitor the performance and availability of cloud-based services and resources.

These tools can provide insights into cloud infrastructure, including virtual machines, storage, and databases, ensuring that cloud-based applications perform optimally.

Endpoint monitoring tools track the performance and security of individual devices, such as laptops, desktops, and mobile devices.

Endpoint monitoring can help organizations detect and remediate security threats on end-user devices.

Infrastructure monitoring tools monitor the health and performance of physical and virtual infrastructure components, including servers, storage, and virtualization platforms.

These tools can help organizations optimize resource utilization and prevent infrastructure-related outages.

Database monitoring tools focus on the performance and availability of database systems, ensuring that databases function efficiently and deliver reliable data access.

Website monitoring tools continuously monitor the availability and performance of websites and web applications, providing insights into user experiences and response times.

Packet capture and analysis tools are used to capture and analyze network traffic at a granular level.

These tools are essential for troubleshooting network issues, diagnosing network problems, and investigating security incidents.

End-user experience monitoring (EUEM) tools focus on measuring the quality of end-user interactions with applications.

EUEM tools can simulate user interactions and capture data on user experiences, helping organizations improve application usability.

Open-source monitoring tools provide cost-effective alternatives to commercial monitoring solutions.

These tools are often highly customizable and can be adapted to specific organizational needs.

Agent-based monitoring tools require the installation of monitoring agents on monitored systems.

These agents collect and transmit data to a centralized monitoring server, allowing for detailed and real-time monitoring.

Agentless monitoring tools do not require the installation of monitoring agents.

Instead, they use existing protocols and interfaces to gather data from remote systems, reducing the overhead associated with agent deployment.

Hybrid monitoring solutions combine both agent-based and agentless monitoring techniques to provide comprehensive insights into an organization's IT environment.

Automation and orchestration are increasingly integrated into monitoring tools, allowing for automated responses to detected issues and the execution of predefined workflows.

Machine learning and artificial intelligence (AI) are used in some monitoring tools to analyze historical data and identify patterns, anomalies, and potential performance or security issues.

Scalability is a crucial consideration when selecting monitoring tools, as organizations must ensure that their chosen solution can accommodate the growing complexity and scale of their IT environment.

Integration capabilities are also important, as monitoring tools should be able to integrate with other IT management and security solutions to provide a holistic view of the organization's IT operations.

Comprehensive reporting and analytics are essential features of monitoring tools, enabling IT teams to generate customized reports, visualize data, and make informed decisions based on historical performance and security data.

In summary, monitoring tools and techniques are indispensable for organizations looking to maintain the performance, availability, and security of their IT environments.

These tools cover a wide range of areas, including performance, security, network, and application monitoring, and come in various forms, from real-time dashboards to log analysis solutions.

The choice of monitoring tools should align with an organization's specific needs, scale, and goals, ensuring that it can effectively manage and protect its IT assets in an ever-evolving technological landscape.

Developing effective incident response plans is a critical aspect of cybersecurity for organizations of all sizes and industries.

These plans outline the steps and procedures to follow when a cybersecurity incident occurs, helping organizations minimize damage and recover swiftly.

An incident response plan begins with defining the objectives of the plan, which typically include the identification, containment, eradication, and recovery from security incidents. It's essential to establish clear and specific goals for incident response, ensuring that everyone involved understands their role and responsibilities.

One of the first steps in developing an incident response plan is forming an incident response team, consisting of members from various departments, such as IT, legal, communications, and management.

This team should include individuals with technical expertise in cybersecurity, as well as those who can handle legal and public relations aspects of an incident.

The incident response team's leader, often referred to as the incident commander, plays a crucial role in coordinating the response efforts and making key decisions during an incident.

Once the team is in place, the next step is to define the types of incidents that the plan will address.

Common incident categories include malware infections, data breaches, denial of service attacks, insider threats, and more.

Each incident category may require a different response strategy, so it's essential to have predefined procedures for each.

Incident classification is a critical aspect of an incident response plan, as it helps prioritize responses based on the severity and impact of the incident.

Organizations often use a classification system, such as a severity scale, to categorize incidents and determine the appropriate level of response.

The plan should also specify how incidents will be reported, including who should report them and what information should be included in the initial incident report.

Timely reporting is crucial to initiating a swift response and containment efforts.

A key element of an incident response plan is defining the roles and responsibilities of each team member and outlining their specific tasks during an incident.

Roles may include incident commander, technical analysts, legal counsel, public relations, and communication coordinators.

Responsibilities should be clear and concise to avoid confusion during high-stress situations.

An essential component of incident response planning is establishing communication procedures and protocols.

This includes defining how the incident response team communicates internally and externally, with stakeholders, law enforcement, and regulatory bodies.

Effective communication is vital for coordinating response efforts and maintaining transparency during an incident.

Incident detection and containment procedures are critical for minimizing the impact of security incidents.

The plan should specify how the incident response team will detect and confirm incidents, including the use of monitoring tools and security alerts.

Containment procedures should detail how the team will isolate affected systems or networks to prevent further damage or data loss.

Eradication and recovery strategies should be outlined in the incident response plan, including how the organization will eliminate the root cause of the incident and restore affected systems to normal operation.

This may involve restoring data from backups, patching vulnerabilities, and implementing security improvements.

Legal and regulatory compliance is a critical consideration in incident response planning.

The plan should specify how the organization will comply with legal requirements, such as data breach notification laws, and how it will preserve evidence for potential legal actions.

Additionally, the plan should address the organization's obligations regarding reporting incidents to regulatory authorities.

Public relations and communication strategies are essential components of an incident response plan.

The plan should detail how the organization will communicate with affected parties, such as customers, employees, and business partners, as well as the media and the public.

Clear and timely communication is crucial for maintaining trust and minimizing reputational damage.

Testing and exercising the incident response plan is a vital step in its development.

Regular tabletop exercises and simulated incident scenarios help the incident response team practice their roles and identify areas for improvement.

The plan should specify how often these exercises will be conducted and how they will be evaluated and documented.

Documentation and record-keeping are essential throughout the incident response process.

The plan should outline what information needs to be documented during an incident, including incident reports, actions taken, and lessons learned.

This documentation is valuable for post-incident analysis and for making improvements to the plan.

Continuous improvement is a key principle in incident response planning.

The plan should include a process for reviewing and updating the plan regularly to reflect changes in technology, threats, and the organization's structure.

This ensures that the plan remains relevant and effective over time.

Collaboration with external resources, such as incident response providers, law enforcement, and cybersecurity experts, should also be addressed in the plan.

The organization should establish relationships and communication channels with these resources to enhance incident response capabilities.

Finally, it's essential to educate and train employees on the incident response plan and their roles in the event of an incident.

Regular training and awareness programs help ensure that employees are prepared to respond effectively when an incident occurs.

In summary, developing an effective incident response plan is a critical component of an organization's cybersecurity strategy.

The plan should define objectives, establish an incident response team, classify incidents, outline roles and responsibilities, detail communication procedures, and address legal and regulatory compliance.

Testing and continuous improvement are essential to ensure that the plan remains effective in the face of evolving threats.

Chapter 7: Becoming a Cybersecurity Ninja

Achieving expertise in cybersecurity is a journey that requires dedication, continuous learning, and a deep understanding of the evolving threat landscape.

Cybersecurity is a dynamic field, and experts in this domain must stay up-to-date with the latest techniques, technologies, and vulnerabilities to effectively protect organizations from cyber threats.

Becoming an expert in cybersecurity often begins with a strong foundation in information technology, computer science, or a related field.

A solid understanding of networking, operating systems, and programming languages is essential for tackling complex security challenges.

Aspiring cybersecurity experts should also cultivate a strong curiosity and a hacker mindset, which involves thinking like a cybercriminal to anticipate and mitigate potential threats.

One of the fundamental building blocks of cybersecurity expertise is gaining knowledge in various security domains.

These domains encompass areas such as network security, application security, cloud security, cryptography, and incident response.

Mastery of these domains allows cybersecurity professionals to address a wide range of security concerns effectively.

To gain expertise in cybersecurity, individuals often pursue relevant certifications, such as Certified Information Systems Security Professional (CISSP), Certified Ethical Hacker (CEH), Certified Information Security Manager (CISM), or Certified Information Security Auditor (CISA).

These certifications validate skills and knowledge in specific areas of cybersecurity and can open doors to career opportunities.

Cybersecurity experts must continuously expand their knowledge by staying informed about emerging threats and vulnerabilities.

They should regularly read industry publications, research reports, and security blogs to understand the latest attack techniques and trends.

Staying connected with the cybersecurity community through forums, conferences, and professional organizations is also invaluable for knowledge sharing and networking.

Hands-on experience is a crucial component of expertise in cybersecurity.

Cybersecurity professionals should seek opportunities to work on real-world security projects, conduct penetration testing, and participate in incident response activities.

Practical experience provides valuable insights and hones the skills needed to address security challenges effectively.

Understanding the psychology of cybercriminals and their motivations is an often-overlooked aspect of cybersecurity expertise.

Cybersecurity professionals should study the tactics, techniques, and procedures (TTPs) employed by attackers to better anticipate and defend against their actions.

Threat intelligence plays a vital role in staying ahead of cyber threats.

Cybersecurity experts should leverage threat intelligence feeds and platforms to gather information on emerging threats, indicators of compromise (IoCs), and attack patterns.

This intelligence can inform proactive security measures and threat hunting efforts.

Security automation and orchestration are increasingly important skills for cybersecurity experts.

Automating routine security tasks and orchestrating incident response workflows can significantly enhance an organization's ability to respond to threats efficiently.

Ethical hacking, also known as penetration testing, is a critical skill for cybersecurity professionals.

It involves simulating cyberattacks to identify vulnerabilities and weaknesses in an organization's systems and applications.

Ethical hackers must think creatively and adapt their techniques to uncover potential security flaws.

Understanding the legal and ethical aspects of cybersecurity is paramount for experts in this field.

Cybersecurity professionals must adhere to strict ethical guidelines and legal frameworks to ensure their activities are within the boundaries of the law.

Privacy and data protection laws, such as the General Data Protection Regulation (GDPR), must be followed diligently.

Communication and collaboration skills are essential for cybersecurity experts.

They need to convey complex technical concepts to non-technical stakeholders and collaborate effectively with various teams within an organization.

Cybersecurity is a multidisciplinary field, and experts often work alongside IT teams, legal departments, and senior management to address security concerns.

Security incident response is a critical area of expertise for cybersecurity professionals.

The ability to detect, analyze, and mitigate security incidents, including data breaches and cyberattacks, is essential for minimizing damage and protecting an organization's reputation.

Continuous improvement is a fundamental principle for cybersecurity experts.

They should regularly assess their skills and seek opportunities for professional development.

Participating in training programs and workshops, pursuing advanced certifications, and seeking mentorship from experienced professionals can all contribute to expertise growth.

An important aspect of cybersecurity expertise is the ability to develop and implement comprehensive security strategies.

Cybersecurity experts must assess an organization's specific risks and design tailored security measures to address those risks effectively.

This involves creating security policies, procedures, and controls to safeguard digital assets.

In the constantly evolving world of cybersecurity, experts should be proactive in identifying emerging technologies and trends.

They should assess how these developments may impact an organization's security posture and adapt accordingly.

As part of their expertise, cybersecurity professionals must develop a deep understanding of the technologies and tools available for threat detection and prevention.

They should be able to evaluate and select the most appropriate security solutions to meet an organization's unique needs.

Mentorship is a valuable resource for aspiring cybersecurity experts.

Seeking guidance from experienced professionals can provide valuable insights, career advice, and opportunities for growth.

Many cybersecurity experts attribute their success to the mentorship they received throughout their careers.

Ultimately, achieving expertise in cybersecurity is an ongoing process that requires a combination of education, experience, and a commitment to continuous improvement.

Cybersecurity experts play a crucial role in protecting organizations from a wide range of threats, and their expertise is in high demand in today's digital world.

Navigating career advancement in the field of cybersecurity is a rewarding but challenging endeavor that requires careful planning and continuous self-improvement.

As you progress in your cybersecurity career, you'll find that opportunities for advancement and growth abound, but they often come with increased responsibilities and expectations.

One of the essential steps in advancing your career is setting clear career goals and objectives.

Take the time to assess your current skills, strengths, and areas for improvement, and then define where you want to be in the future.

These goals will serve as your roadmap and guide your career decisions.

Networking plays a vital role in career advancement.

Building strong professional relationships within the cybersecurity community can lead to valuable opportunities, such as job referrals, mentorship, and collaborations on projects.

Attend industry conferences, join professional organizations, and actively participate in online cybersecurity forums to expand your network.

Seeking mentorship from experienced cybersecurity professionals can provide invaluable guidance and insights.

A mentor can help you navigate the complexities of the field, offer career advice, and share their knowledge and experiences.

Identify potential mentors who align with your career goals and reach out to them for guidance.

Continuous learning is a cornerstone of career advancement in cybersecurity.

The field is ever-evolving, with new threats and technologies emerging regularly.

Invest in your education by pursuing certifications, taking relevant courses, and staying up-to-date with the latest developments in cybersecurity.

Specializing in a specific area of cybersecurity can enhance your career prospects.

Consider focusing on areas such as penetration testing, incident response, or cloud security, depending on your interests and career goals.

Becoming an expert in a niche field can make you an invaluable asset to organizations seeking specialized skills.

Developing a well-rounded skillset is also essential.

While specialization is valuable, having a broad understanding of various cybersecurity domains can help you excel in leadership and management roles.

Consider acquiring knowledge in areas like risk management, compliance, and governance.

Effective communication skills are critical for career advancement.

As you move into leadership positions, the ability to convey complex technical information to non-technical stakeholders becomes increasingly important.

Hone your communication skills, both written and verbal, to effectively convey your ideas and strategies.

Leadership and management skills are vital for those aiming for senior roles.

Learning how to lead teams, manage projects, and make strategic decisions is essential for career progression.

Consider enrolling in leadership courses or seeking opportunities to lead cybersecurity initiatives within your organization.

Building a strong professional brand can set you apart in the competitive field of cybersecurity.

Maintain an active online presence by sharing your knowledge through blogs, articles, or social media.

Demonstrate your expertise and showcase your contributions to the cybersecurity community.

Adaptability is a crucial trait for career advancement.

The cybersecurity landscape is constantly evolving, with new technologies, threats, and regulations shaping the industry.

Being open to change and willing to learn new skills will make you more resilient and adaptable in your career.

Consider pursuing advanced degrees, such as a Master's in Cybersecurity or an MBA with a cybersecurity focus, to enhance your qualifications for leadership roles.

Certifications are a valuable asset in the cybersecurity field.

Consider pursuing certifications such as Certified Information Systems Security Professional (CISSP), Certified Information Security Manager (CISM), or Certified Ethical Hacker (CEH) to demonstrate your expertise to potential employers and advance your career.

Taking on challenging projects and seeking opportunities to lead cybersecurity initiatives within your organization can showcase your skills and dedication.

Demonstrate your ability to tackle complex problems and deliver results that positively impact the organization's security posture.

Developing a strong professional network within your organization is essential for career advancement.

Seek out opportunities to collaborate with colleagues from different departments and showcase your expertise in cybersecurity.

A track record of successful collaborations can lead to promotions and increased responsibilities.

Consider pursuing opportunities for public speaking or presenting at industry events.

Sharing your knowledge and insights with a broader audience can raise your profile in the cybersecurity community and open doors for career advancement.

It's essential to stay current with industry trends and news.

Subscribe to cybersecurity publications, follow industry blogs, and attend webinars and conferences to keep abreast of the latest developments in the field.

Mentoring others can be a fulfilling aspect of career advancement.

As you gain experience and expertise, consider offering guidance and mentorship to junior cybersecurity professionals. This not only benefits others but also reinforces your own knowledge and leadership skills.

A commitment to ethical conduct and professionalism is crucial for career advancement.

Maintain high ethical standards, adhere to legal and regulatory requirements, and prioritize the protection of sensitive information.

Ethical behavior is valued in the cybersecurity field and can enhance your reputation.

In summary, navigating career advancement in the field of cybersecurity requires a combination of strategic planning, continuous learning, networking, and leadership development.

Setting clear goals, specializing in a niche area, and building a strong professional brand can propel your career forward.

Maintain adaptability and a commitment to ethical conduct to ensure long-term success in this dynamic and ever-changing field.

Chapter 8: Ethical Hacking and Offensive Security

The role of ethical hackers in cybersecurity is pivotal to proactively identify vulnerabilities and secure digital environments.

These professionals, also known as white-hat hackers, use their expertise to assess the security posture of organizations, applications, and systems.

Ethical hackers employ the same techniques as malicious hackers but with the intent of uncovering weaknesses and helping organizations strengthen their defenses.

The primary objective of ethical hacking is to prevent data breaches, protect sensitive information, and safeguard against cyber threats.

Ethical hackers act as the first line of defense against malicious cyberattacks, helping organizations identify and address vulnerabilities before attackers can exploit them.

Their work is essential to maintaining the confidentiality, integrity, and availability of digital assets.

To become ethical hackers, individuals must possess a strong foundation in computer science, networking, and cybersecurity.

They need to understand the techniques used by malicious hackers and stay informed about the latest security threats and vulnerabilities.

Certifications such as Certified Ethical Hacker (CEH) and Offensive Security Certified Professional (OSCP) are often pursued by those entering this field to validate their skills.

Ethical hackers must also adhere to strict ethical guidelines and legal frameworks.

They must obtain proper authorization before conducting security assessments and ensure that their actions are within the boundaries of the law.

Once authorized, ethical hackers employ a variety of methodologies to identify vulnerabilities in an organization's systems.

They conduct penetration testing, which involves simulating cyberattacks to assess the effectiveness of security measures.

During these tests, ethical hackers search for weaknesses in network configurations, web applications, and mobile devices.

They may also use social engineering techniques to assess an organization's susceptibility to phishing attacks and other forms of manipulation.

Vulnerability assessment tools and automated scanners are frequently used by ethical hackers to identify common security issues, such as outdated software, misconfigured systems, and known vulnerabilities.

Once vulnerabilities are identified, ethical hackers provide detailed reports to organizations, outlining their findings and recommendations for remediation.

These reports are essential for organizations to prioritize and address security issues effectively.

Ethical hackers often work closely with IT teams, security professionals, and management to implement necessary security measures.

They may assist in patching vulnerabilities, configuring firewalls, and improving security policies and procedures.

In addition to identifying technical vulnerabilities, ethical hackers assess the human element of security.

They conduct social engineering tests to evaluate an organization's susceptibility to manipulation by attackers.

This includes testing employees' awareness of security best practices, their ability to recognize phishing emails, and their willingness to follow security policies.

Ethical hackers play a critical role in improving an organization's security culture by raising awareness and providing training.

Their assessments help organizations strengthen their security posture and reduce the risk of data breaches and cyberattacks.

One of the challenges ethical hackers face is keeping up with the rapidly evolving threat landscape.

New attack techniques, vulnerabilities, and malware strains are constantly emerging, requiring ethical hackers to adapt and stay ahead of malicious actors.

Continuous learning and staying current with industry trends are essential for success in this field.

Ethical hackers must also maintain the highest levels of professionalism and integrity.

They are entrusted with sensitive information and must handle it with the utmost care and confidentiality.

Ethical hacking is a dynamic and fulfilling career path with numerous opportunities for growth and specialization.

Some ethical hackers choose to focus on specific areas of expertise, such as web application security, mobile device security, or network penetration testing.

This specialization allows them to become experts in their chosen domains and offer specialized services to organizations.

Ethical hackers also contribute to the cybersecurity community by sharing their knowledge and experiences.

They often participate in cybersecurity forums, conferences, and online communities, where they collaborate with peers and exchange information about emerging threats and best practices.

Mentoring and educating the next generation of ethical hackers is another valuable contribution to the field.

Many professionals in this field take on mentorship roles to guide newcomers and help them develop the necessary skills and ethical mindset.

In summary, ethical hackers play a critical role in cybersecurity by proactively identifying and addressing vulnerabilities to protect organizations from cyber threats.

Their expertise, ethical conduct, and dedication to improving security make them invaluable assets in the ongoing battle against malicious hackers.

Offensive security strategies for defending networks are an essential component of a comprehensive cybersecurity approach.

While defensive measures are crucial for protecting networks, offensive strategies involve actively testing and assessing network security from the perspective of an attacker.

These offensive tactics help organizations identify weaknesses and vulnerabilities before malicious hackers can exploit them.

One of the primary offensive security strategies is penetration testing, which involves simulating cyberattacks to assess network vulnerabilities.

During a penetration test, security professionals, often referred to as ethical hackers or pen testers, attempt to exploit weaknesses in the network's defenses.

This process allows organizations to identify and remediate vulnerabilities proactively.

Penetration testers use a variety of techniques to assess network security, including scanning for open ports, searching for misconfigured devices, and attempting to gain unauthorized access.

The goal is to uncover vulnerabilities that could be exploited by malicious actors.

Red teaming is another offensive security strategy that goes beyond penetration testing.

In red team exercises, a dedicated team of experts, known as the red team, simulates a real-world cyberattack.

Their mission is to infiltrate the network, breach security defenses, and achieve specific objectives, such as accessing sensitive data or compromising critical systems.

This approach provides a more comprehensive assessment of an organization's security posture by testing its ability to detect and respond to sophisticated attacks.

Offensive security strategies also encompass vulnerability assessment and management.

Regularly scanning network assets for vulnerabilities and prioritizing their remediation is essential for maintaining a secure network.

Vulnerability assessment tools help identify weaknesses in software, hardware, and configurations.

Once vulnerabilities are identified, organizations can prioritize their remediation efforts based on the severity of the issues and the potential impact on the network.

Ethical hacking is a core component of offensive security strategies.

Ethical hackers, also known as white-hat hackers, use their skills to assess network security from the perspective of an attacker.

They perform security assessments, conduct penetration tests, and attempt to exploit vulnerabilities with the organization's consent.

The insights gained from ethical hacking activities enable organizations to strengthen their defenses and reduce the risk of successful cyberattacks.

Offensive security strategies also involve conducting social engineering assessments.

Social engineering is a technique used by malicious hackers to manipulate individuals into divulging sensitive information or taking actions that compromise security.

Ethical hackers may conduct phishing simulations or other social engineering tests to assess an organization's susceptibility to these types of attacks.

These assessments help organizations improve employee awareness and training programs.

Effective network segmentation is another offensive strategy for enhancing network security.

Segmentation divides a network into smaller, isolated segments, limiting lateral movement for attackers who gain access to one segment.

By implementing strong access controls and segmentation, organizations can contain breaches and prevent attackers from moving freely within the network.

Intrusion detection and prevention systems (IDS/IPS) are crucial tools in offensive security.

These systems monitor network traffic for suspicious activities and patterns that may indicate an ongoing cyberattack.

IDS/IPS can detect and block malicious traffic, preventing potential threats from compromising network security.

Honeypots and honeynets are offensive security techniques designed to attract and trap malicious actors.

Honeypots are decoy systems or resources deliberately exposed to the internet to lure attackers.

When an attacker targets a honeypot, security teams can gain valuable insights into their tactics and tools.

Honeynets expand on this concept by creating entire simulated network environments to attract and study attackers' activities.

By analyzing the behavior of attackers in these controlled environments, organizations can improve their defenses and threat intelligence.

Offensive security strategies also encompass the use of threat intelligence.

Threat intelligence provides organizations with information about the latest cyber threats, including attack techniques, malware, and known threat actors.

This information enables organizations to proactively adjust their security measures to counter emerging threats.

Bug bounty programs are a proactive approach to offensive security.

Organizations offer monetary rewards to security researchers who discover and responsibly disclose vulnerabilities in their systems or applications.

These programs encourage external experts to help identify and remediate security issues.

The offensive security landscape is dynamic, and organizations must continuously adapt their strategies to address evolving threats.

Regularly conducting security assessments and staying current with industry trends and best practices are essential for maintaining a strong defensive posture.

While offensive security strategies play a vital role in network defense, they should be conducted with care and under strict ethical guidelines.

All offensive activities should be conducted with the organization's full knowledge and consent to avoid any potential legal or ethical issues.

In summary, offensive security strategies are a critical component of defending networks against cyber threats.

By proactively identifying vulnerabilities and weaknesses, organizations can strengthen their security posture and reduce the risk of successful cyberattacks.

Ethical hacking, penetration testing, vulnerability assessments, and other offensive techniques are essential tools for maintaining a secure and resilient network.

Chapter 9: Securing the Cloud and Virtual Environments

Cloud security considerations are paramount in today's digital landscape, as organizations increasingly rely on cloud services to store and manage their data and applications.

The adoption of cloud computing offers numerous benefits, including scalability, cost-efficiency, and flexibility, but it also introduces unique security challenges.

To effectively secure data and applications in the cloud, organizations must carefully evaluate and address these considerations.

One fundamental cloud security consideration is data protection.

Sensitive data stored in the cloud, whether in a public, private, or hybrid cloud environment, must be encrypted both in transit and at rest to prevent unauthorized access.

Encryption ensures that even if a malicious actor gains access to the data, it remains unreadable without the appropriate encryption keys.

Another crucial aspect of cloud security is identity and access management (IAM).

Organizations must implement robust IAM policies and practices to control who has access to cloud resources and what actions they can perform.

Implementing strong authentication mechanisms, such as multi-factor authentication (MFA), enhances the security of user accounts.

The principle of least privilege should guide access controls, ensuring that users and applications have only the permissions necessary for their tasks.

Configuration management is a critical consideration in cloud security.

Misconfigured cloud resources are a common source of data breaches and security incidents.

Organizations must carefully configure cloud services and resources to align with security best practices.

Implementing automation and cloud security tools can help organizations identify and rectify misconfigurations quickly.

Continuous monitoring and auditing are essential for cloud security.

Organizations should implement robust logging and monitoring solutions to track user activities, access to resources, and security events in the cloud environment.

Regularly reviewing and analyzing these logs can help detect suspicious activities and security incidents promptly.

Security Information and Event Management (SIEM) systems are valuable tools for aggregating and analyzing log data.

Compliance with regulatory requirements and industry standards is a significant cloud security consideration.

Many organizations are subject to specific data protection regulations, such as GDPR, HIPAA, or PCI DSS, which have implications for how they handle data in the cloud.

Ensuring compliance with these requirements is essential to avoid legal and financial consequences.

Cloud service providers play a crucial role in cloud security.

Organizations should carefully evaluate the security practices and certifications of their chosen cloud providers.

Leading cloud providers typically undergo rigorous security audits and offer a range of security features and services.

However, organizations must still take responsibility for securing their data and applications within the cloud.

Data residency and sovereignty are important considerations for organizations operating in a global context.

Different regions and countries may have varying data protection laws and requirements.

Organizations should be aware of where their cloud data is stored and ensure compliance with relevant data sovereignty regulations.

The shared responsibility model is a fundamental concept in cloud security.

Under this model, cloud service providers are responsible for the security of the cloud infrastructure, while customers are responsible for securing their data and applications within that infrastructure.

Understanding and defining the boundaries of this shared responsibility is critical for effective cloud security.

Secure development practices are essential for cloud applications.

Organizations must integrate security into the development lifecycle of their cloud-based applications, from design to deployment.

Performing code reviews, vulnerability assessments, and security testing can help identify and address security flaws before they become exploitable weaknesses.

The use of containers and container orchestration platforms in the cloud introduces its own set of security considerations.

Organizations must secure container images, ensure proper access controls, and monitor containerized applications for vulnerabilities and runtime security.

Cloud-native security solutions and best practices are essential for protecting cloud-native applications effectively.

The evolving threat landscape requires organizations to stay current with emerging threats and vulnerabilities.

Regularly updating security policies and practices to address new risks is vital.

Threat intelligence feeds and security information sharing communities can provide valuable insights into the latest threats and attack techniques.

Cloud security should extend beyond the technical aspects and include security awareness and training for employees.

Educating users about security best practices, phishing awareness, and the risks associated with cloud services can help mitigate human-related security incidents.

Disaster recovery and business continuity planning are integral to cloud security.

Organizations should have robust plans in place to recover data and applications in the event of a cloud outage or security breach.

Regularly testing these plans ensures their effectiveness.

Incident response planning is critical for minimizing the impact of security incidents in the cloud.

Organizations must have well-defined incident response procedures, including communication protocols, incident containment strategies, and legal and regulatory reporting processes.

Cloud security considerations extend to third-party vendors and partners that have access to an organization's cloud resources or data.

Vetting the security practices of third parties and establishing contractual agreements for security responsibilities are crucial steps in mitigating potential risks.

In summary, cloud security considerations are multifaceted and require a holistic approach to protect data and applications in the cloud effectively.

Encryption, IAM, configuration management, compliance, and continuous monitoring are all essential components of a robust cloud security strategy.

Organizations must also consider shared responsibility, secure development practices, container security, and cloud-native security to address the evolving threat landscape comprehensively.

Furthermore, security awareness, disaster recovery planning, incident response, and third-party security assessments are critical aspects of cloud security that organizations should prioritize to safeguard their digital assets effectively.

Virtualization security is a critical concern in modern IT environments as organizations increasingly rely on virtualization technologies to optimize resource utilization and streamline operations.

Virtualization allows multiple virtual machines (VMs) to run on a single physical server, providing flexibility, scalability, and cost-efficiency, but it also introduces unique security challenges.

To ensure the security of virtualized environments, organizations must adopt best practices and employ robust security measures.

One of the primary concerns in virtualization security is the isolation of VMs.

VMs share the same physical hardware, but effective isolation mechanisms must be in place to prevent one VM from compromising the security of others.

Hypervisors, the software that manages and controls VMs, play a crucial role in maintaining this isolation.

It is essential to choose a hypervisor with a strong security track record and to keep it regularly updated.

Another vital aspect of virtualization security is patch management.

VMs, like physical servers, require regular updates and patches to address vulnerabilities.

Failure to keep VMs up-to-date can leave them susceptible to known exploits.

Organizations must establish a robust patch management process to ensure that all VMs are promptly updated with the latest security patches.

Security policies and access controls must be consistently enforced in virtualized environments.

VMs should only be accessible to authorized users and systems, and the principle of least privilege should guide access rights.

Role-based access control (RBAC) and strong authentication mechanisms are essential for managing VM access effectively.

Encryption is critical in virtualization security to protect data at rest and in transit within VMs.

Organizations should implement encryption technologies to safeguard sensitive information within VMs and while it is transferred between VMs.

Virtual network security is a significant concern in virtualized environments.

Organizations should employ network segmentation to isolate different groups of VMs and prevent lateral movement of threats.

Firewalls and intrusion detection systems (IDS) or intrusion prevention systems (IPS) should be deployed to monitor and protect virtualized network traffic.

Auditing and monitoring are essential for identifying suspicious activities and potential security incidents in virtualized environments.

Security information and event management (SIEM) solutions can aggregate and analyze log data from VMs, hypervisors, and other virtualization components.

Regularly reviewing these logs can help detect unauthorized access, abnormal behavior, and potential security threats.

Ensuring the integrity of VM images is a critical consideration.

VM images should be created from trusted sources and should undergo regular integrity checks to identify any unauthorized modifications or tampering.

Secure boot mechanisms can help guarantee the integrity of the boot process for VMs.

A robust backup and disaster recovery strategy is essential for virtualization security.

Organizations must ensure that VMs are regularly backed up, and recovery processes are tested to minimize downtime and data loss in case of a security incident or hardware failure.

Virtualization-specific security solutions can provide additional layers of protection.

These solutions offer features such as memory introspection, hypervisor-based firewalls, and advanced threat detection specifically designed for virtualized environments.

Security awareness and training are essential components of virtualization security.

IT staff and users must be educated about the unique security considerations of virtualized environments, including the risks associated with VM sprawl and overprovisioning.

Physical security of the data center housing the virtualized infrastructure is also critical.

Unauthorized physical access to servers or storage devices can compromise the security of VMs.

Organizations must implement stringent physical security measures, including access controls and surveillance, to protect the physical hardware.

Regular security assessments and audits of the virtualized environment are vital for identifying and addressing security weaknesses.

External security experts or internal security teams should conduct penetration tests and vulnerability assessments to evaluate the effectiveness of security measures.

Virtualization security is an ongoing process that requires continuous monitoring and adaptation to emerging threats and vulnerabilities.

Organizations should stay informed about the latest virtualization security best practices and keep their virtualization technologies up-to-date.

The adoption of cloud-based virtualization solutions introduces additional security considerations.

Organizations must carefully evaluate the security controls and practices of cloud providers when deploying virtualized resources in the cloud.

In summary, virtualization security is essential to protect the integrity, availability, and confidentiality of data and applications in virtualized environments.

Robust isolation mechanisms, patch management, access controls, encryption, network security, auditing, and monitoring are all critical components of a comprehensive virtualization security strategy.

Additionally, ensuring the integrity of VM images, implementing backup and disaster recovery, and staying informed about emerging threats are essential practices to safeguard virtualized environments effectively.

Chapter 10: Staying Ahead of Emerging Cyber Threats

Anticipating future cyber threats is a constant challenge in the ever-evolving landscape of cybersecurity.

Cyber threats continue to evolve, becoming more sophisticated and adaptable, making it essential for organizations to stay ahead of potential risks.

One crucial aspect of anticipating future cyber threats is understanding the motivations and goals of threat actors.

These actors may include cybercriminals, nation-states, hacktivists, and insiders with malicious intent.

By analyzing their motives, organizations can better predict the types of attacks they may face.

Financial gain, espionage, disruption, and political objectives are common motivations for cyberattacks.

Understanding these motives helps organizations anticipate the likely targets and tactics used by threat actors.

Technological advancements play a significant role in shaping future cyber threats.

Emerging technologies such as artificial intelligence, quantum computing, and the Internet of Things (IoT) introduce new attack surfaces and vulnerabilities.

As these technologies become more widespread, organizations must anticipate the potential security risks they pose.

Zero-day vulnerabilities, which are previously unknown and unpatched vulnerabilities in software and hardware, are a perpetual concern in cybersecurity.

Cyber attackers often exploit these vulnerabilities before they are discovered and patched.

To anticipate future threats, organizations must invest in vulnerability research and threat intelligence to detect zero-day vulnerabilities and prepare for potential exploits.

The growing interconnectivity of systems and devices also presents challenges in anticipating cyber threats.

As more devices become interconnected, the attack surface expands, offering attackers more entry points.

This interconnectedness includes critical infrastructure, industrial control systems, and smart cities, making them potential targets for cyberattacks.

Understanding the potential impact of attacks on these interconnected systems is crucial for threat anticipation.

The dark web and underground forums are places where cybercriminals exchange tools, tactics, and information about potential targets.

Monitoring these platforms can provide valuable insights into upcoming cyber threats, including new attack techniques and malware.

Organizations can use this information to prepare for potential attacks and strengthen their defenses.

Nation-state actors pose a significant threat in the cybersecurity landscape.

These well-funded and highly skilled groups often engage in espionage, cyberwarfare, and sabotage.

Anticipating future nation-state cyber threats requires a deep understanding of geopolitical tensions and global events that may trigger cyberattacks.

Advanced persistent threats (APTs) are a type of cyber threat that remains hidden within a target's network for an extended period, often with the intent of stealing sensitive data.

To anticipate APTs, organizations must invest in continuous monitoring, anomaly detection, and threat hunting to identify and mitigate threats early in their lifecycle.

Social engineering attacks, such as phishing, spear-phishing, and pretexting, remain effective tactics for cybercriminals.

Anticipating future social engineering threats involves educating employees and implementing strong security awareness programs.

As technology evolves, the human element remains a vulnerability that attackers can exploit.

Artificial intelligence (AI) and machine learning (ML) are double-edged swords in cybersecurity.

While they can be used to detect and mitigate threats, they can also be leveraged by attackers to automate and enhance their attacks.

To anticipate future AI-driven cyber threats, organizations must invest in AI and ML capabilities for threat detection and response.

Supply chain attacks are increasingly common, where attackers compromise the software or hardware supply chain to infiltrate target organizations.

To anticipate and defend against supply chain attacks, organizations should assess the security practices of their suppliers and implement robust supply chain security measures.

Ransomware attacks have grown in frequency and sophistication, with attackers targeting critical infrastructure, healthcare, and government organizations.

To anticipate future ransomware threats, organizations should implement effective backup and recovery strategies, regularly update security measures, and consider the potential consequences of paying ransoms.

Nation-state-sponsored cyber-espionage campaigns often use advanced techniques to steal sensitive information.

Anticipating these threats involves monitoring for signs of unauthorized access, exfiltration of data, and suspicious network activities.

Cybersecurity professionals must remain vigilant and adapt to the evolving threat landscape.

Continuous learning, threat intelligence sharing, and collaboration with other organizations and law enforcement agencies are essential for anticipating and mitigating future cyber threats.

In summary, anticipating future cyber threats is an ongoing and challenging process that requires a deep understanding of threat actors' motivations, technological advancements, interconnected systems, and emerging attack techniques.

Organizations must invest in threat intelligence, vulnerability research, monitoring, and employee training to stay ahead of potential threats and protect their digital assets effectively.

By anticipating and preparing for future cyber threats, organizations can enhance their cybersecurity posture and minimize the impact of potential attacks.

Preparing for emerging cybersecurity challenges is a critical endeavor for organizations in today's fast-paced digital landscape.

As technology continues to advance, so do the tactics and techniques of cyber adversaries, making it essential for cybersecurity professionals to proactively address potential threats.

One of the most significant emerging cybersecurity challenges is the increasing sophistication of cyberattacks.

Attackers are continually developing new methods to bypass security measures, making it difficult for organizations to stay ahead of the curve.

To prepare for these advanced threats, organizations should invest in cutting-edge security technologies and continuously update their cybersecurity strategies.

The rise of artificial intelligence and machine learning in cybersecurity presents both opportunities and challenges.

While AI can enhance threat detection and response, it can also be exploited by attackers to automate attacks.

Organizations should embrace AI-driven cybersecurity solutions while remaining vigilant against potential AI-driven threats.

The Internet of Things (IoT) introduces a new dimension to cybersecurity challenges.

As more devices become connected to the internet, the attack surface expands, providing cybercriminals with additional entry points.

To prepare for IoT-related threats, organizations should implement robust security measures for IoT devices and networks.

The remote and hybrid work models adopted in response to the COVID-19 pandemic have also created cybersecurity challenges.

With more employees working from home, organizations must ensure that remote access is secure and that employees are trained in cybersecurity best practices.

Ransomware attacks have surged in recent years, targeting organizations of all sizes and industries.

Preparing for ransomware threats involves developing robust backup and recovery strategies, implementing security awareness training, and regularly patching and updating systems to prevent vulnerabilities.

Supply chain attacks have become a prominent concern, where attackers compromise the software or hardware supply chain to infiltrate target organizations.

To prepare for supply chain threats, organizations should assess the security practices of their suppliers and establish strict supply chain security measures.

Cloud security remains a critical concern as more organizations migrate their data and applications to the cloud.

Preparing for cloud security challenges involves understanding the shared responsibility model, implementing strong access controls, and monitoring cloud environments for unusual activities.

The evolving regulatory landscape adds complexity to cybersecurity preparations.

Organizations must comply with various data protection regulations, such as GDPR and CCPA, and prepare for potential legal and financial consequences of non-compliance.

Cybersecurity professionals face a shortage of skilled talent, making it challenging to fill critical roles.

To address this challenge, organizations should invest in cybersecurity training and education for their existing workforce and actively recruit new talent.

The increasing interconnectedness of systems and devices creates a ripple effect in cybersecurity.

A breach or compromise in one area can quickly spread to other parts of the network, highlighting the importance of network segmentation and containment strategies.

Preparing for emerging cybersecurity challenges also involves building a resilient cybersecurity culture within an organization.

Employees should be trained to recognize and report security incidents promptly, fostering a proactive approach to cybersecurity.

Regularly conducting tabletop exercises and simulations can help prepare the organization for potential cyber incidents.

Cybersecurity threat intelligence sharing is a valuable practice for staying informed about emerging threats.

Organizations should collaborate with industry peers, government agencies, and threat intelligence providers to gain insights into evolving cyber threats.

Continual assessment and improvement of security measures are essential for staying ahead of emerging threats.

Organizations should conduct regular security assessments, penetration tests, and vulnerability scans to identify weaknesses and take corrective actions.

Investing in advanced threat detection and response capabilities, such as Security Information and Event Management (SIEM) systems, can help organizations proactively detect and mitigate emerging threats.

Finally, cybersecurity preparedness requires a comprehensive incident response plan.

Organizations should have well-defined incident response procedures, communication protocols, and legal and regulatory reporting processes in place.

Regularly testing and updating the incident response plan ensures its effectiveness in mitigating the impact of cybersecurity incidents.

In summary, preparing for emerging cybersecurity challenges is an ongoing and multifaceted effort that requires organizations to adapt and evolve continuously.

By addressing advanced threats, embracing new technologies, securing IoT devices, and staying compliant with regulations, organizations can enhance their cybersecurity posture.

Fostering a culture of cybersecurity awareness, sharing threat intelligence, and investing in talent and incident response capabilities are critical steps in preparing for the cybersecurity challenges of the future.

BOOK 4
CYBERWATCH UNLEASHED
EXPERT STRATEGIES FOR SAFEGUARDING YOUR DIGITAL
WORLD
ROB BOTWRIGHT

Chapter 1: The Evolving Landscape of Cyber Threats

A historical overview of cyber threats reveals a complex and evolving landscape of digital vulnerabilities and attacks.

The roots of cyber threats can be traced back to the early days of computer technology when the concept of hacking emerged. In the 1960s and 1970s, hackers were often individuals who explored computer systems out of curiosity and a desire to understand their inner workings.

However, as technology advanced, so did the motivations behind cyber threats.

In the 1980s, cyberattacks began to take on more malicious forms with the emergence of viruses and worms.

One of the earliest and most notorious examples was the Morris Worm, unleashed by Robert Tappan Morris in 1988, which infected thousands of computers and caused widespread disruption.

The 1990s witnessed a proliferation of cyber threats, including the rise of malware, denial-of-service attacks, and the spread of computer viruses.

The "ILOVEYOU" worm in 2000 was a notable example that caused significant damage and financial losses worldwide.

During this decade, cybercriminals began to exploit the internet for financial gain, targeting online banking and e-commerce.

As the 21st century dawned, cyber threats became more sophisticated and financially motivated.

Phishing attacks, where attackers impersonate trusted entities to steal sensitive information, gained prominence.

One of the largest and most famous data breaches occurred in 2013 when hackers compromised Target's point-of-sale system, exposing millions of customers' credit card information.

The cyber threat landscape continued to evolve with the emergence of advanced persistent threats (APTs) linked to nation-states.

State-sponsored actors engaged in cyber-espionage and cyber-attacks against other nations, targeting critical infrastructure, government agencies, and private companies.

The Stuxnet worm, discovered in 2010, was a groundbreaking example of state-sponsored cyber warfare, designed to disrupt Iran's nuclear program.

Ransomware attacks gained notoriety in the mid-2010s, with threats like CryptoLocker and WannaCry encrypting victims' data and demanding ransoms for decryption keys.

These attacks affected individuals, businesses, and even entire municipalities, highlighting the profitability of ransomware for cybercriminals.

The Internet of Things (IoT) introduced a new dimension to cyber threats, as interconnected devices created more entry points for attackers.

In 2016, the Mirai botnet targeted vulnerable IoT devices, launching massive distributed denial-of-service (DDoS) attacks against websites and online services.

Social engineering attacks, such as spear-phishing and business email compromise (BEC), became prevalent, exploiting human vulnerabilities rather than technical weaknesses.

By impersonating trusted individuals or organizations, cybercriminals tricked victims into divulging sensitive information or transferring funds.

The SolarWinds cyberattack in 2020 exemplified the level of sophistication that APTs could achieve.

Russian state-sponsored hackers compromised SolarWinds' software updates, infiltrating thousands of organizations, including government agencies and Fortune 500 companies.

The attack highlighted the vulnerability of the software supply chain.

In recent years, cyber threats have expanded to include not only financial motivations but also political, ideological, and geopolitical objectives.

Hacktivist groups, like Anonymous, have targeted governments, corporations, and organizations to promote their causes and ideologies.

Cyber threats have also extended into the realm of critical infrastructure, with potential consequences for public safety.

Incidents like the Colonial Pipeline ransomware attack in 2021 underscored the vulnerability of essential systems to cyberattacks.

The rise of cryptocurrencies has facilitated cybercriminal activities, as ransom payments can be made more anonymously.

Cryptocurrency-enabled ransomware attacks have proliferated, with attackers demanding payments in cryptocurrencies like Bitcoin.

The COVID-19 pandemic accelerated the shift to remote work, creating new opportunities for cybercriminals.

Phishing attacks related to COVID-19, fraudulent vaccine offers, and remote desktop protocol (RDP) vulnerabilities exploited during the pandemic underscored the adaptability of cyber threats.

Cyber threats continue to evolve with the emergence of artificial intelligence and machine learning technologies.

These tools can be leveraged by attackers to automate attacks and evade detection.

To combat these evolving threats, organizations must invest in advanced cybersecurity technologies, threat intelligence, and employee training.

The historical overview of cyber threats highlights the persistent and dynamic nature of cybersecurity challenges.

As technology advances, new threats will emerge, and organizations must remain vigilant, proactive, and adaptable to protect their digital assets and information.

The interconnectedness of the digital world, the proliferation of IoT devices, and the potential for state-sponsored cyber warfare all underscore the importance of cybersecurity in the modern age.

Cybersecurity is not just a technical challenge; it is a critical aspect of national security, economic stability, and individual privacy.

Emerging threat trends and challenges in the field of cybersecurity are continuously reshaping the landscape of digital security.

As technology advances, so do the tactics and techniques employed by cyber adversaries, requiring constant vigilance and adaptation from organizations and security professionals.

One notable emerging threat trend is the increasing sophistication of ransomware attacks.

Cybercriminals are using advanced encryption methods and tactics to target organizations of all sizes, including critical infrastructure, healthcare facilities, and local governments.

These attacks often lead to significant financial losses and operational disruptions.

Another concerning trend is the rise of supply chain attacks, where attackers compromise software or hardware vendors to infiltrate target organizations.

The SolarWinds incident in 2020 highlighted the devastating impact such attacks can have on national security and private industry.

Phishing attacks remain a pervasive challenge, with attackers using increasingly convincing lures to trick individuals into divulging sensitive information or installing malware.

Spear-phishing, in particular, targets specific individuals within organizations and can lead to data breaches or financial fraud.

The growth of the Internet of Things (IoT) introduces new security challenges, as interconnected devices expand the attack surface.

Weaknesses in IoT security can result in large-scale botnets and distributed denial-of-service (DDoS) attacks, disrupting online services and websites.

Social engineering attacks, such as business email compromise (BEC), continue to target employees and organizations.

Attackers use social engineering tactics to manipulate individuals into taking actions that compromise security or lead to financial losses.

The expansion of remote work due to the COVID-19 pandemic has created opportunities for cybercriminals to exploit vulnerabilities in remote access solutions and employee behavior.

Security professionals must ensure that remote access is secure and that employees are educated about cybersecurity best practices.

State-sponsored cyberattacks pose a significant threat, as nation-states engage in cyber-espionage, cyber-warfare, and the targeting of critical infrastructure.

These attacks often involve advanced persistent threats (APTs) and require organizations to maintain high levels of vigilance and readiness.

Emerging technologies like artificial intelligence (AI) and machine learning (ML) present both opportunities and challenges for cybersecurity.

While they can enhance threat detection and response, they can also be used by attackers to automate and enhance their attacks.

The adoption of cryptocurrencies has facilitated cybercriminal activities, as they provide a level of anonymity for ransom payments.

Cryptocurrency-enabled ransomware attacks have become increasingly prevalent, making it challenging to trace and apprehend cybercriminals.

The convergence of physical and digital security is another emerging trend, as cyber threats can have real-world consequences.

Attacks on critical infrastructure, healthcare systems, and smart cities have the potential to impact public safety and well-being.

The evolving regulatory landscape adds complexity to cybersecurity challenges, as organizations must navigate a web of data protection and privacy regulations.

Non-compliance can result in legal and financial consequences, requiring organizations to invest in compliance efforts.

Cybersecurity professionals face a persistent shortage of skilled talent, making it challenging to fill critical roles.

To address this challenge, organizations should invest in cybersecurity education and training for their workforce and actively recruit new talent.

The concept of zero trust security, which assumes that no one, whether inside or outside the organization, can be trusted by default, is gaining traction as a security model.

This approach requires strict access controls and continuous authentication to mitigate the risk of insider threats and external attacks.

Emerging threats also extend to the cloud, as more organizations migrate their data and applications to cloud environments.

Securing cloud assets requires a shared responsibility model, with organizations responsible for securing their data and configurations within the cloud.

The convergence of operational technology (OT) and information technology (IT) networks in critical infrastructure sectors presents unique challenges.

Cyberattacks on OT systems can have far-reaching consequences, making it essential to establish robust security measures and incident response plans.

Threat intelligence sharing among organizations, government agencies, and industry groups is crucial for staying informed about emerging threats.

Collaborative efforts can help identify and mitigate threats more effectively.

Investing in advanced threat detection and response capabilities, such as Security Information and Event Management (SIEM) systems, is essential for proactive threat mitigation.

Regularly conducting security assessments, penetration tests, and vulnerability scans helps identify and address weaknesses in an organization's security posture.

Incident response plans should be well-defined and regularly tested to ensure their effectiveness in mitigating the impact of cybersecurity incidents.

In summary, emerging threat trends and challenges continue to reshape the cybersecurity landscape, requiring organizations and security professionals to remain adaptable and proactive.

As technology evolves, new threats will arise, making it essential to invest in advanced security technologies, threat intelligence, and employee training.

The interconnected nature of digital systems, the proliferation of IoT devices, and the potential for state-sponsored cyber warfare all emphasize the importance of cybersecurity in the modern age.

Cybersecurity is not merely a technical concern; it is a critical aspect of national security, economic stability, and individual privacy, demanding continuous attention and investment.

Chapter 2: Mastering Advanced Threat Detection

Advanced threat detection technologies play a crucial role in safeguarding digital environments from a myriad of evolving cyber threats.

In today's complex cybersecurity landscape, traditional signature-based approaches are no longer sufficient to detect sophisticated and novel threats.

To address this challenge, organizations have turned to advanced threat detection technologies that leverage cutting-edge techniques and methodologies.

One of the key components of advanced threat detection is machine learning, which enables systems to analyze vast amounts of data and identify patterns that may indicate potential threats.

Machine learning algorithms can continuously adapt and improve their detection capabilities based on real-time data, making them highly effective in uncovering previously unseen threats.

Anomaly detection is a prominent application of machine learning in advanced threat detection.

By establishing a baseline of normal network or user behavior, anomaly detection algorithms can identify deviations that may indicate suspicious activities.

Behavioral analytics is another crucial aspect of advanced threat detection, which focuses on monitoring user and entity behavior to detect signs of compromise.

By analyzing user activities and their interactions with digital assets, behavioral analytics can pinpoint subtle anomalies that might evade traditional detection methods.

Intrusion detection systems (IDS) have evolved into more advanced forms, such as network-based IDS (NIDS) and host-based IDS (HIDS), which offer enhanced threat detection capabilities.

NIDS monitors network traffic for unusual patterns and signatures, while HIDS examines the activities and configurations of individual host systems.

A newer development is the use of deception technology in advanced threat detection.

Deception solutions create decoy assets, such as fake servers and files, to lure attackers into revealing themselves.

These decoys can help security teams detect and respond to threats early in the attack lifecycle.

Endpoint detection and response (EDR) solutions have become increasingly sophisticated, offering real-time monitoring, threat hunting capabilities, and automated response actions.

EDR tools can analyze endpoint activities to identify suspicious behaviors and quickly contain threats.

Security information and event management (SIEM) systems have evolved to support advanced threat detection by correlating and analyzing data from various sources, providing security teams with a comprehensive view of their environment.

SIEM platforms can apply machine learning algorithms to identify anomalous patterns indicative of security incidents.

Cloud-based advanced threat detection services have gained popularity, as organizations migrate their workloads and data to cloud environments.

These services can offer advanced threat detection and response capabilities tailored to cloud-based infrastructure and applications.

Threat intelligence feeds and feeds from external sources have become integral to advanced threat detection strategies.

By incorporating threat intelligence feeds, organizations can stay informed about the latest threat indicators, tactics, techniques, and procedures (TTPs) used by cyber adversaries.

Advanced threat detection technologies often include automated incident response capabilities, allowing security teams to respond rapidly to threats as they are detected.

Automated responses may include isolating compromised endpoints, blocking malicious traffic, or initiating predefined remediation steps.

To enhance the effectiveness of advanced threat detection technologies, organizations are adopting a holistic and integrated approach to security.

This approach involves the integration of various security tools and technologies, enabling them to work together to detect, investigate, and respond to threats more efficiently.

Threat hunting, performed by skilled security analysts, complements advanced threat detection technologies by proactively searching for signs of compromise that may evade automated detection.

By combining human expertise with advanced tools, threat hunting can uncover sophisticated threats that might otherwise go unnoticed.

Endpoint detection and response (EDR) solutions have become increasingly sophisticated, offering real-time monitoring, threat hunting capabilities, and automated response actions.

EDR tools can analyze endpoint activities to identify suspicious behaviors and quickly contain threats.

Security information and event management (SIEM) systems have evolved to support advanced threat detection by correlating and analyzing data from various sources, providing security teams with a comprehensive view of their environment.

SIEM platforms can apply machine learning algorithms to identify anomalous patterns indicative of security incidents.

Cloud-based advanced threat detection services have gained popularity, as organizations migrate their workloads and data to cloud environments.

These services can offer advanced threat detection and response capabilities tailored to cloud-based infrastructure and applications.

Threat intelligence feeds and feeds from external sources have become integral to advanced threat detection strategies.

By incorporating threat intelligence feeds, organizations can stay informed about the latest threat indicators, tactics, techniques, and procedures (TTPs) used by cyber adversaries.

Advanced threat detection technologies often include automated incident response capabilities, allowing security teams to respond rapidly to threats as they are detected.

Automated responses may include isolating compromised endpoints, blocking malicious traffic, or initiating predefined remediation steps.

To enhance the effectiveness of advanced threat detection technologies, organizations are adopting a holistic and integrated approach to security.

This approach involves the integration of various security tools and technologies, enabling them to work together to detect, investigate, and respond to threats more efficiently.

Threat hunting, performed by skilled security analysts, complements advanced threat detection technologies by proactively searching for signs of compromise that may evade automated detection.

By combining human expertise with advanced tools, threat hunting can uncover sophisticated threats that might otherwise go unnoticed.

Threat intelligence and threat hunting are two essential practices in the field of cybersecurity, each playing a unique role in enhancing an organization's security posture.

Threat intelligence involves the collection, analysis, and dissemination of information about cyber threats and vulnerabilities.

This information can come from a variety of sources, including open-source feeds, commercial threat intelligence providers, government agencies, and internal data.

The goal of threat intelligence is to provide organizations with insights into potential threats that may target their systems, applications, or data.

One of the key benefits of threat intelligence is its ability to help organizations understand the tactics, techniques, and procedures (TTPs) employed by cyber adversaries.

By analyzing threat intelligence, security teams can gain a better understanding of the motives and capabilities of potential attackers.

Threat intelligence can be categorized into several types, including strategic, operational, and tactical intelligence.

Strategic intelligence focuses on high-level, long-term threats and trends, helping organizations make informed decisions about their overall security strategy.

Operational intelligence is more specific and addresses ongoing threats and attacks, while tactical intelligence provides real-time information about immediate threats and incidents.

To effectively leverage threat intelligence, organizations must establish processes for collecting, analyzing, and applying this information to their security operations.

Security teams often use threat intelligence feeds to receive automated updates about known threats and indicators of compromise (IoCs).

By integrating threat intelligence into their security infrastructure, organizations can enhance their ability to detect and respond to threats promptly.

While threat intelligence is crucial for proactive threat mitigation, threat hunting takes a more proactive and hands-on approach to identifying threats.

Threat hunting involves the active search for signs of compromise or malicious activity within an organization's network and endpoints.

Unlike traditional security measures that rely on predefined rules and signatures, threat hunting is guided by the hypothesis that threats may exist within the environment, even if they have not triggered alarms or alerts.

Threat hunters, often skilled security analysts, use their expertise to explore data, logs, and network traffic to uncover hidden threats that automated systems might miss.

This proactive approach allows organizations to identify and remediate threats before they escalate into significant security incidents.

Threat hunting often involves the use of advanced tools and technologies, such as security information and event management (SIEM) systems, to analyze large datasets for anomalies and suspicious patterns.

It also requires a deep understanding of an organization's infrastructure and a willingness to explore the unknown.

Threat hunters follow a hypothesis-driven process, starting with a question or theory about potential threats and then gathering and analyzing data to validate or refute their assumptions.

The goal of threat hunting is to identify threats that may have gone undetected by automated security measures, such as advanced persistent threats (APTs) and insider threats.

Threat intelligence and threat hunting are complementary practices that work together to strengthen an organization's cybersecurity defenses.

Threat intelligence provides valuable information about known threats and emerging trends, helping organizations prepare and adapt their security strategies.

Threat hunting, on the other hand, allows organizations to actively search for hidden threats and vulnerabilities within their networks, reducing the dwell time of threats and minimizing their impact.

To establish effective threat intelligence and threat hunting capabilities, organizations should consider several best practices.

First, they should define clear objectives and goals for both practices, aligning them with their overall cybersecurity strategy.

Second, organizations should invest in the necessary technology and tools to collect, analyze, and act on threat intelligence effectively.

This may include the use of threat intelligence platforms and threat hunting solutions.

Third, organizations should establish a dedicated threat intelligence team or designate individuals responsible for threat hunting.

These individuals should receive proper training and have access to the resources needed to perform their roles effectively.

Collaboration and information sharing with industry peers and threat intelligence sharing communities can also enhance an organization's threat intelligence capabilities.

Finally, organizations should continuously assess and refine their threat intelligence and threat hunting processes to adapt to evolving threats and challenges.

In summary, threat intelligence and threat hunting are essential components of modern cybersecurity strategies.

Threat intelligence provides valuable insights into known and emerging threats, while threat hunting proactively seeks out hidden threats within an organization's environment.

By combining these two practices, organizations can improve their ability to detect, respond to, and mitigate cyber threats effectively.

Chapter 3: A Deep Dive into Cybersecurity Frameworks

Understanding frameworks like NIST (National Institute of Standards and Technology) and ISO 27001 is crucial for organizations aiming to establish robust information security management systems.

These frameworks provide guidelines, best practices, and standards for managing and securing sensitive information and data assets.

NIST, a U.S. government agency, plays a significant role in developing cybersecurity and information security standards and guidelines.

The NIST Cybersecurity Framework, in particular, is widely adopted and offers a structured approach to managing and reducing cybersecurity risks.

This framework comprises five core functions: Identify, Protect, Detect, Respond, and Recover.

The Identify function involves understanding and managing the organization's cybersecurity risk by identifying critical assets, vulnerabilities, and potential threats.

The Protect function focuses on implementing safeguards and security measures to protect critical assets from cybersecurity threats.

The Detect function emphasizes the continuous monitoring and detection of cybersecurity incidents and threats.

The Respond function addresses the organization's capability to respond effectively to security incidents when they occur.

The Recover function focuses on the organization's ability to recover from security incidents and restore normal operations.

NIST also provides detailed guidelines and standards for specific areas of cybersecurity, such as encryption, access control, and risk assessment.

ISO 27001, on the other hand, is an international standard for information security management systems (ISMS).

ISO 27001 provides a systematic and risk-based approach to managing information security within an organization.

The standard defines a comprehensive set of controls, policies, and procedures that organizations can implement to protect their information assets.

ISO 27001 is based on a Plan-Do-Check-Act (PDCA) cycle, which is a continuous improvement framework for managing and improving ISMS.

The Plan phase involves establishing the ISMS, defining security policies, conducting risk assessments, and setting security objectives.

The Do phase involves implementing the security controls, training employees, and raising awareness about information security.

The Check phase focuses on monitoring and reviewing the effectiveness of the ISMS through regular audits and assessments.

The Act phase involves taking corrective actions to address any identified deficiencies and continually improving the ISMS.

One of the key advantages of ISO 27001 is its flexibility and adaptability to various industries and organizations of different sizes.

It provides a structured framework that can be tailored to meet the specific needs and risk profiles of individual organizations.

To achieve ISO 27001 certification, organizations must undergo a formal audit process conducted by accredited certification bodies.

The audit evaluates the organization's compliance with the standard's requirements and the effectiveness of its ISMS.

Both NIST and ISO 27001 share common goals, such as protecting sensitive information, managing cybersecurity risks, and ensuring business continuity.

However, they differ in their scope, focus, and applicability.

NIST's frameworks and guidelines are primarily designed for U.S. federal agencies and organizations that interact with the government.

While NIST is widely recognized and used globally, ISO 27001 is an internationally recognized standard applicable to organizations worldwide.

Organizations often use NIST's Cybersecurity Framework to align with ISO 27001 and other international standards.

This alignment helps organizations meet regulatory requirements and improve their cybersecurity posture.

For example, organizations can map NIST's functions (Identify, Protect, Detect, Respond, and Recover) to ISO 27001's PDCA cycle, creating a comprehensive approach to information security.

By implementing a combination of NIST and ISO 27001 best practices, organizations can achieve a higher level of cybersecurity maturity and resilience.

It's important to note that compliance with NIST guidelines or ISO 27001 does not guarantee immunity from cyberattacks or security breaches.

Cyber threats are continually evolving, and organizations must maintain a proactive and adaptive approach to cybersecurity.

Regular risk assessments, threat intelligence, and incident response plans are essential components of a robust cybersecurity strategy.

In summary, understanding frameworks like NIST and ISO 27001 is vital for organizations seeking to establish effective information security management systems.

These frameworks provide valuable guidance and standards for managing and mitigating cybersecurity risks.

By aligning NIST and ISO 27001 best practices, organizations can enhance their cybersecurity posture and better protect their sensitive information and data assets.

Implementing a comprehensive cybersecurity framework is

essential for organizations of all sizes and industries in today's digital landscape.

Such a framework provides a structured approach to safeguarding sensitive data, protecting critical assets, and managing cybersecurity risks.

A well-designed framework serves as a strategic roadmap for organizations to establish, maintain, and continually improve their cybersecurity posture.

The implementation process begins with a thorough assessment of an organization's current cybersecurity state, including its existing policies, procedures, and technologies.

This assessment helps identify vulnerabilities, threats, and areas of improvement.

One widely adopted cybersecurity framework is the NIST Cybersecurity Framework, developed by the National Institute of Standards and Technology.

The NIST Cybersecurity Framework comprises five core functions: Identify, Protect, Detect, Respond, and Recover.

The "Identify" function focuses on understanding the organization's assets, their vulnerabilities, and potential cybersecurity threats.

This involves creating an inventory of hardware, software, data, and personnel, as well as assessing risks and establishing a risk management strategy.

The "Protect" function involves implementing safeguards to prevent or mitigate potential cybersecurity threats.

This includes access controls, encryption, secure configurations, and employee training.

The "Detect" function emphasizes continuous monitoring and early detection of cybersecurity incidents.

Organizations should have mechanisms in place to identify and alert on any suspicious activities or breaches.

The "Respond" function outlines procedures to contain, mitigate, and recover from cybersecurity incidents.

An effective response plan should include steps to notify stakeholders, investigate the incident, and take corrective actions.

Finally, the "Recover" function addresses the restoration of normal operations after a cybersecurity incident.

This includes data recovery, system restoration, and improvements to prevent future incidents.

Implementing the NIST Cybersecurity Framework involves aligning an organization's cybersecurity practices with these five core functions.

Organizations should tailor the framework to meet their specific needs and risk profiles, taking into account industry regulations and best practices.

Another widely used framework is ISO 27001, an international standard for information security management systems (ISMS).

ISO 27001 provides a systematic approach to managing information security risks, ensuring the confidentiality, integrity, and availability of sensitive information.

The implementation of ISO 27001 involves a series of steps, starting with a formal risk assessment and the development of an ISMS policy.

Organizations must establish controls and safeguards to protect information assets, including access controls, encryption, and incident response procedures.

Regular audits and assessments are essential to monitor the effectiveness of the ISMS and identify areas for improvement.

One of the key advantages of ISO 27001 is its adaptability to various industries and organizations.

It provides a flexible framework that can be tailored to meet specific business needs and regulatory requirements.

Implementing a comprehensive cybersecurity framework also requires a strong commitment from top management and an organization-wide culture of security.

Cybersecurity is not solely the responsibility of the IT department but involves all employees, from executives to frontline staff.

Employee training and awareness programs are crucial components of an effective cybersecurity strategy.

In addition to the NIST Cybersecurity Framework and ISO 27001, there are industry-specific frameworks and regulations that organizations must consider.

For example, healthcare organizations must adhere to the Health Insurance Portability and Accountability Act (HIPAA), while financial institutions must comply with the Payment Card Industry Data Security Standard (PCI DSS).

These regulations come with specific requirements and guidelines that organizations must incorporate into their cybersecurity frameworks.

Implementing a comprehensive cybersecurity framework also involves investing in the right technologies and tools.

This includes firewalls, intrusion detection systems, antivirus software, and security information and event management (SIEM) solutions.

Regular software patching and updates are essential to address known vulnerabilities and weaknesses.

Furthermore, organizations must establish an incident response plan that outlines how to handle security incidents when they occur.

This plan should define roles and responsibilities, communication procedures, and steps for containment and recovery.

Testing and simulating incidents through tabletop exercises can help ensure that the response plan is effective.

Continuous monitoring of network traffic and system logs is critical for detecting and responding to potential threats promptly.

Security teams should have access to real-time threat intelligence and collaborate with external organizations and industry groups to stay informed about emerging threats.

Implementing a comprehensive cybersecurity framework is an ongoing process that requires continuous improvement and adaptation to evolving threats.

Organizations should regularly assess their cybersecurity practices, conduct risk assessments, and update their frameworks accordingly.

Engaging with external cybersecurity experts and conducting penetration testing can help identify vulnerabilities and weaknesses.

Finally, organizations must communicate their cybersecurity policies and practices to their employees, customers, and partners.

Transparency builds trust and ensures that all stakeholders are aware of the organization's commitment to cybersecurity.

In summary, implementing a comprehensive cybersecurity framework is essential in today's digital world.

Frameworks like the NIST Cybersecurity Framework and ISO 27001 provide structured approaches to managing and mitigating cybersecurity risks.

By tailoring these frameworks to their specific needs, organizations can establish strong cybersecurity postures, protect sensitive data, and respond effectively to security incidents.

Chapter 4: Advanced Cryptography and Secure Communications

Advanced cryptographic algorithms are at the heart of modern information security, providing the foundation for securing data and communications in an increasingly digital world.

These algorithms play a crucial role in protecting sensitive information, ensuring privacy, and safeguarding against unauthorized access.

Cryptographic algorithms rely on complex mathematical operations to transform plaintext data into ciphertext, rendering it unreadable to anyone without the proper decryption key.

One of the most fundamental cryptographic algorithms is the Advanced Encryption Standard (AES), widely recognized for its security and efficiency.

AES operates on blocks of data and is symmetric, meaning the same key is used for both encryption and decryption.

It offers a range of key lengths, including 128, 192, and 256 bits, providing varying levels of security.

AES encryption is used extensively in various applications, including securing communications over the internet and encrypting files and data at rest.

Another essential cryptographic algorithm is the Rivest Cipher (RC), which includes several variations such as RC4, RC5, and RC6.

RC4, for instance, is a symmetric stream cipher known for its simplicity and speed.

However, RC4 has been found to have vulnerabilities over the years, and its use has become discouraged.

RC5 and RC6 are block ciphers designed to address some of the limitations of earlier versions.

Cryptographic algorithms are also classified into two categories: symmetric and asymmetric.

Symmetric algorithms use the same key for both encryption and decryption, while asymmetric algorithms use a pair of keys – a public key for encryption and a private key for decryption.

The most widely used asymmetric cryptographic algorithm is the RSA algorithm, named after its inventors, Ron Rivest, Adi Shamir, and Leonard Adleman.

RSA relies on the mathematical properties of large prime numbers and modular arithmetic, making it secure for encrypting data and establishing secure communication channels.

One of the key advantages of RSA is its role in digital signatures, which verify the authenticity and integrity of digital documents and messages.

Elliptic Curve Cryptography (ECC) is another important asymmetric algorithm gaining popularity due to its strong security properties and efficiency.

ECC is particularly suitable for resource-constrained devices like smartphones and Internet of Things (IoT) devices, where computational power and memory are limited.

The Diffie-Hellman key exchange is a fundamental cryptographic protocol used to establish a shared secret key between two parties over an unsecured network.

It relies on the computational difficulty of solving the discrete logarithm problem, making it secure against eavesdroppers.

The Diffie-Hellman protocol forms the basis for many secure communication protocols, including Transport Layer Security (TLS) used for secure web browsing.

Hash functions are another critical component of modern cryptographic algorithms.

Hash functions take an input (or message) and produce a fixed-size output called a hash value or digest.

These hash values are unique for different inputs, and even a small change in the input results in a significantly different hash value.

This property ensures the integrity of data and provides a way to verify that data has not been tampered with during transmission or storage.

The Secure Hash Algorithm (SHA) family, including SHA-256 and SHA-3, is widely used for generating hash values.

Cryptographic algorithms are continually evolving to stay ahead of emerging threats and computing capabilities.

Post-Quantum Cryptography (PQC) is an active research area focused on developing cryptographic algorithms that remain secure against attacks from quantum computers.

Quantum computers have the potential to break many of the commonly used cryptographic algorithms today, such as RSA and ECC, due to their ability to perform certain mathematical calculations exponentially faster.

To address this threat, researchers are exploring new cryptographic algorithms based on different mathematical principles, such as lattice-based cryptography and code-based cryptography.

Lattice-based cryptography, in particular, shows promise as a post-quantum solution because it relies on the computational complexity of problems in high-dimensional lattices.

These problems are believed to be resistant to quantum attacks, making lattice-based cryptography a strong candidate for securing data in a post-quantum world.

In summary, advanced cryptographic algorithms are essential for securing data, communications, and information systems in the digital age.

They rely on complex mathematical operations, symmetric and asymmetric key management, and hash functions to provide confidentiality, integrity, and authenticity.

As quantum computing advances, post-quantum cryptography is becoming increasingly important to ensure the long-term security of information in a rapidly evolving technological landscape.

Researchers and practitioners in the field of cryptography continue to innovate and develop robust cryptographic algorithms to protect sensitive information and enable secure digital interactions.

Secure communication protocols are the foundation of secure digital interactions in today's interconnected world, ensuring that data exchanged between parties remains confidential and protected from eavesdropping and tampering.

These protocols play a critical role in safeguarding sensitive information, such as personal messages, financial transactions, and sensitive business data.

Insecure communication can expose individuals and organizations to significant risks, including data breaches, identity theft, and financial losses.

Secure communication protocols use a combination of cryptographic techniques, authentication methods, and security measures to establish and maintain secure channels for data exchange.

One of the most widely used secure communication protocols is Transport Layer Security (TLS), formerly known as Secure Sockets Layer (SSL).

TLS encrypts data as it travels between a client and a server, ensuring that even if intercepted by malicious actors, the data remains unreadable without the appropriate decryption key.

TLS is the backbone of secure web browsing, protecting online shopping, banking, and other sensitive transactions.

Another essential secure communication protocol is the Internet Protocol Security (IPsec), which operates at the network layer to secure data exchanged between devices within a network.

IPsec provides a framework for encryption and authentication, ensuring the confidentiality and integrity of data as it traverses the internet or private networks.

Virtual Private Networks (VPNs) often rely on IPsec to create secure tunnels for remote access and secure communications between networks.

For securing email communications, Pretty Good Privacy (PGP) and its open-source counterpart, GNU Privacy Guard (GPG), offer end-to-end encryption and digital signatures.

PGP and GPG use public and private key pairs to encrypt and decrypt messages, ensuring that only the intended recipient can read the contents of an email.

Secure communication protocols also play a vital role in securing voice and video calls over the internet.

The Secure Real-time Transport Protocol (SRTP) is specifically designed for protecting the confidentiality and integrity of real-time media streams, making it essential for secure voice and video communication.

Instant messaging and chat applications have become integral to modern communication, and secure protocols like the Off-the-Record Messaging (OTR) protocol ensure that these conversations remain private and tamper-proof.

OTR uses end-to-end encryption and forward secrecy to protect instant messages from eavesdropping and decryption in the future, even if an encryption key is compromised.

Another secure communication protocol for chat applications is the Signal Protocol, which is known for its robust security and widespread adoption in messaging apps like Signal, WhatsApp, and Facebook Messenger.

Signal Protocol provides end-to-end encryption for text messages, voice calls, and video calls, ensuring that only the intended recipients can access the content of these conversations.

Secure communication protocols extend beyond the realm of internet-based applications and are also crucial for securing communication within private networks.

The Simple Network Management Protocol version 3 (SNMPv3) enhances SNMP security by providing authentication and encryption mechanisms, protecting against unauthorized access and tampering of network management data.

For secure file transfer within networks, the Secure File Transfer Protocol (SFTP) and the Secure Shell (SSH) protocol are widely used.

SFTP and SSH use encryption and authentication to protect data transfer and remote access to network resources, preventing unauthorized access and data interception.

In the realm of wireless communication, the Wi-Fi Protected Access (WPA) and WPA2 protocols ensure the security of Wi-Fi networks by encrypting data transmitted between devices and access points.

These protocols have been widely adopted to protect the confidentiality of wireless communications and prevent unauthorized access to Wi-Fi networks.

Secure communication protocols are continuously evolving to address emerging threats and vulnerabilities.

For example, the latest version of TLS, TLS 1.3, improves security by removing older, less secure encryption algorithms and providing faster handshake processes.

TLS 1.3 also enhances forward secrecy, further protecting data even if encryption keys are compromised.

The adoption of secure communication protocols is not limited to businesses and organizations; individuals also benefit from these protocols in their everyday digital interactions.

When sending a sensitive email, making an online purchase, or accessing a bank account, individuals rely on secure communication protocols to safeguard their personal and financial information.

To ensure the effectiveness of secure communication protocols, it is essential to keep them up to date with the latest security patches and adhere to best practices for their implementation.

Additionally, user awareness and education play a crucial role in preventing security breaches and ensuring that individuals and organizations use these protocols correctly.

In summary, secure communication protocols are the backbone of secure digital interactions in our interconnected world.

They protect data confidentiality, integrity, and authenticity, safeguarding sensitive information from eavesdropping, tampering, and unauthorized access.

From web browsing to email, voice and video calls to instant messaging, secure communication protocols are integral to our daily lives, enabling us to communicate and transact online with confidence and peace of mind.

Chapter 5: Protecting Critical Infrastructure

Securing critical infrastructure is of paramount importance in today's interconnected and digitized world, as these systems and facilities are vital to the functioning of society and the economy.

Critical infrastructure encompasses a wide range of sectors, including energy, transportation, water supply, telecommunications, healthcare, and more, each requiring unique security measures tailored to its specific needs.

The protection of critical infrastructure involves a multifaceted approach that addresses physical security, cybersecurity, and risk management.

Physical security measures for critical infrastructure begin with controlling access to sensitive areas and facilities.

Access control includes methods such as perimeter fencing, security gates, access badges, and biometric authentication to ensure that only authorized personnel can enter secure areas.

In addition to access control, video surveillance and intrusion detection systems are crucial tools for monitoring and responding to physical threats.

These systems provide real-time alerts and evidence collection capabilities to deter and detect unauthorized access and potential security breaches.

Critical infrastructure operators also employ security personnel, such as guards and surveillance teams, to maintain a physical presence and respond to security incidents promptly.

Another vital aspect of physical security is the protection of critical infrastructure against natural disasters, accidents, and acts of terrorism.

Facility hardening involves designing and constructing infrastructure to withstand extreme weather events, seismic activity, and other potential hazards.

Furthermore, contingency plans and emergency response protocols must be in place to address unexpected incidents and minimize their impact.

While physical security measures are essential, the digital realm is equally critical in securing critical infrastructure.

Cybersecurity measures are vital to protect critical infrastructure systems from cyberattacks, which can have devastating consequences.

Cybersecurity begins with identifying vulnerabilities and weaknesses in the infrastructure's digital components, such as industrial control systems (ICS), supervisory control and data acquisition (SCADA) systems, and internet-connected devices.

Regular vulnerability assessments and penetration testing help identify and address these weaknesses before they can be exploited by malicious actors.

Firewalls, intrusion detection systems (IDS), and intrusion prevention systems (IPS) are deployed to monitor and filter network traffic, preventing unauthorized access and cyberattacks.

Network segmentation is a crucial cybersecurity measure that separates critical infrastructure networks into isolated zones, limiting the lateral movement of cyber threats.

Secure authentication and authorization protocols, such as multi-factor authentication (MFA) and role-based access control (RBAC), ensure that only authorized personnel can access critical systems.

Encryption is another critical cybersecurity measure, protecting data both in transit and at rest.

Encryption ensures that even if data is intercepted by cybercriminals, it remains unreadable without the appropriate decryption keys.

Security patches and updates must be applied promptly to all software and hardware components of critical infrastructure systems to address known vulnerabilities.

Regular cybersecurity training and awareness programs for employees and personnel are essential in preventing social engineering attacks, such as phishing, which often target individuals with access to critical systems.

Moreover, continuous monitoring and threat intelligence sharing with government agencies and industry peers help identify and respond to emerging cyber threats effectively.

Beyond physical and cybersecurity measures, critical infrastructure operators must adopt robust risk management practices.

Risk assessments are conducted to identify potential threats and vulnerabilities, assess their potential impact, and prioritize security measures accordingly.

These assessments help organizations allocate resources and develop a comprehensive security strategy.

Business continuity and disaster recovery plans are essential components of risk management, ensuring that critical infrastructure can continue to operate during and after a security incident or natural disaster.

Regular drills and exercises help test and improve these plans, ensuring a swift and coordinated response in times of crisis.

Collaboration with government agencies, law enforcement, and other stakeholders is essential to enhance security measures for critical infrastructure.

Information sharing and coordination enable a more comprehensive understanding of threats and vulnerabilities, facilitating a collective response to emerging security challenges.

Regulatory frameworks and standards play a significant role in guiding security measures for critical infrastructure.

Many countries have established regulations and standards specific to critical infrastructure sectors, outlining security requirements and compliance measures.

Compliance with these regulations is crucial to ensure that critical infrastructure operators meet minimum security standards and protect against potential threats.

Additionally, international standards, such as ISO 27001 for information security management and NIST Cybersecurity Framework, provide valuable guidelines for enhancing cybersecurity measures.

Investing in research and development is another essential aspect of securing critical infrastructure.

Innovative technologies, such as artificial intelligence (AI), machine learning, and blockchain, can strengthen security measures by enhancing threat detection, authentication, and data integrity.

Moreover, threat modeling and scenario analysis help anticipate and prepare for emerging threats, allowing critical infrastructure operators to stay one step ahead of potential adversaries.

In summary, securing critical infrastructure is a complex and multifaceted endeavor that requires a combination of physical security measures, robust cybersecurity practices, risk management, and collaboration with various stakeholders.

Protecting critical infrastructure is essential not only for the stability and security of a nation but also for the well-being of its citizens and the continuity of essential services.

By implementing comprehensive security measures and staying vigilant against evolving threats, critical infrastructure operators can safeguard these vital systems and ensure their resilience in the face of both physical and digital challenges.

Case studies in critical infrastructure protection provide valuable insights into real-world challenges and solutions, offering a deeper understanding of the complexities involved in safeguarding vital systems.

One such case study focuses on the cybersecurity breach of a major electric utility company's infrastructure.

In this instance, a state-sponsored hacking group successfully infiltrated the utility's network, gaining unauthorized access to critical systems.

The breach highlighted the vulnerability of critical infrastructure to cyberattacks and underscored the importance of robust cybersecurity measures.

The hackers' objective was to disrupt the power grid, potentially causing widespread blackouts and chaos.

Fortunately, the utility company had implemented an advanced intrusion detection system that detected the breach in its early stages.

This early detection allowed the company's security team to respond swiftly, isolate the compromised systems, and prevent any further infiltration.

The incident emphasized the critical role of intrusion detection systems in identifying and mitigating cyber threats to critical infrastructure.

Another case study examines a targeted physical attack on a water treatment facility.

In this scenario, a group of individuals with insider knowledge of the facility gained access to its premises.

They tampered with the water purification process, introducing harmful chemicals that could have contaminated the entire water supply.

The incident exposed the need for enhanced physical security measures, including stringent access controls and employee background checks.

Additionally, it emphasized the importance of monitoring and surveillance to detect unauthorized access and suspicious activities within critical infrastructure facilities.

A third case study involves a coordinated attack on a major transportation hub.

In this instance, a group of cybercriminals targeted the control systems of a busy airport, seeking to disrupt flight operations and compromise passenger safety.

The attackers exploited vulnerabilities in the airport's operational technology (OT) systems, gaining control over critical components such as air traffic control and baggage handling.

The incident raised concerns about the convergence of IT and OT systems in critical infrastructure and the need for comprehensive cybersecurity strategies that encompass both domains.

Moreover, it highlighted the potential cascading effects of a cyberattack on critical infrastructure, affecting not only the facility but also the broader economy and public safety.

In another case study, a sophisticated ransomware attack targeted a healthcare organization responsible for managing medical records and patient care systems.

The attack encrypted critical patient data, rendering it inaccessible and disrupting healthcare services.

The incident underscored the significance of data protection and the need for robust backup and recovery solutions in critical infrastructure sectors like healthcare.

The organization was forced to pay a substantial ransom to regain access to its data, emphasizing the financial and operational consequences of cyberattacks on critical infrastructure.

Additionally, the case study highlighted the importance of employee training and awareness to prevent ransomware attacks and other cybersecurity threats.

A final case study examines a natural disaster affecting a major oil refinery.

In this scenario, a severe hurricane struck the coastal region where the refinery was located, causing extensive damage to its infrastructure and disrupting operations.

The incident demonstrated the vulnerability of critical infrastructure to natural disasters and the necessity of disaster preparedness and recovery plans.

The refinery's resilience and ability to recover swiftly were attributed to its comprehensive disaster recovery and continuity planning.

These case studies offer valuable lessons in critical infrastructure protection, illustrating the diverse challenges and solutions encountered in safeguarding essential systems.

They highlight the importance of proactive measures, such as cybersecurity, physical security, access control, and disaster preparedness, in mitigating risks and ensuring the resilience of critical infrastructure.

Moreover, they emphasize the need for continuous monitoring, response readiness, and collaboration among stakeholders, including government agencies, private sector organizations, and the public.

By examining these real-world scenarios, policymakers, security professionals, and critical infrastructure operators can gain valuable insights and apply best practices to enhance the protection of vital systems essential for the well-being and prosperity of nations.

Chapter 6: Offensive Security Techniques for Defense

Offensive security tools and methodologies are essential components of cybersecurity, used to identify vulnerabilities and weaknesses in systems and networks.

These tools and techniques are employed by ethical hackers and security professionals to proactively assess and strengthen the security posture of an organization.

One of the primary offensive security methodologies is penetration testing, commonly referred to as "pen testing."

Penetration testing involves simulating cyberattacks on a target system or network to identify vulnerabilities that could be exploited by malicious actors.

The goal is to find weaknesses before cybercriminals do and provide recommendations for remediation.

Pen testers use a variety of tools and methodologies to conduct their assessments, including network scanners, vulnerability scanners, and exploitation frameworks.

Network scanners, such as Nmap and Nessus, are used to discover hosts, open ports, and services running on a network.

Vulnerability scanners, like OpenVAS and Qualys, assess systems for known vulnerabilities by comparing their configurations and software versions against a database of security flaws.

Exploitation frameworks like Metasploit provide a structured way to test vulnerabilities by automating the process of identifying, exploiting, and gaining access to target systems.

In addition to penetration testing, another offensive security methodology is social engineering testing.

Social engineering involves manipulating individuals into divulging confidential information or performing actions that compromise security.

Phishing, pretexting, baiting, and tailgating are common social engineering techniques.

Phishing attacks, for instance, use deceptive emails to trick recipients into clicking on malicious links or providing sensitive information.

To counter social engineering, organizations conduct awareness training for employees and implement email filtering systems that detect and block phishing attempts.

Another important offensive security tool is Wi-Fi hacking tools used to assess the security of wireless networks.

Tools like Aircrack-ng and Wireshark are employed to test the vulnerability of Wi-Fi networks, including testing the strength of encryption protocols like WPA and WPA2.

This ensures that unauthorized individuals cannot gain unauthorized access to the network.

Web application security testing tools, such as Burp Suite and OWASP ZAP, focus on identifying vulnerabilities in web applications.

They can detect issues like SQL injection, cross-site scripting (XSS), and insecure authentication mechanisms.

By conducting web application assessments, organizations can prevent these vulnerabilities from being exploited by cyber attackers.

For identifying vulnerabilities in mobile applications, security professionals use mobile application security testing tools like MobSF and APKTool.

These tools analyze mobile apps for weaknesses and vulnerabilities that could compromise user data and privacy.

Web application and mobile application security assessments are essential for protecting against attacks targeting these increasingly common attack vectors.

Beyond penetration testing, security professionals often employ adversary emulation tools and methodologies.

Adversary emulation aims to mimic the tactics, techniques, and procedures (TTPs) of real cyber adversaries to test an organization's defensive capabilities.

Tools like Atomic Red Team and MITRE ATT&CK provide resources and frameworks for simulating adversary behavior and testing detection and response mechanisms.

By emulating adversaries, organizations can better understand their own vulnerabilities and enhance their threat detection and response strategies.

In addition to specific offensive security tools and methodologies, ethical hackers and security professionals must also possess a deep understanding of the ethical and legal considerations involved in offensive security testing.

Ethical hacking requires strict adherence to a code of ethics and compliance with relevant laws and regulations.

Permission must be obtained before conducting any offensive security testing on systems or networks that do not belong to the tester.

Failure to do so could result in legal consequences and damage to an organization's reputation.

Additionally, responsible disclosure of vulnerabilities is a fundamental principle in offensive security.

Ethical hackers should report any vulnerabilities they discover to the affected organization promptly and provide guidance on how to remediate them.

This responsible approach ensures that vulnerabilities are addressed before they can be exploited by malicious actors.

In summary, offensive security tools and methodologies play a critical role in assessing and enhancing the security of systems and networks.

Penetration testing, social engineering testing, Wi-Fi hacking tools, web and mobile application security assessments, adversary emulation, and ethical considerations are all integral components of offensive security.

By using these tools and methodologies responsibly and in compliance with ethical and legal standards, organizations can better protect their assets and data from cyber threats.

Ethical hacking, often referred to as "white hat" hacking, is the practice of intentionally probing computer systems, networks, and applications for vulnerabilities and weaknesses with the consent of the owner.

The primary objective of ethical hacking is to identify security flaws and potential entry points that malicious hackers could exploit.

Ethical hackers use their skills and knowledge to strengthen an organization's security posture and protect it from cyber threats.

Ethical hackers operate under a strict code of ethics and legal framework, ensuring that their activities remain within the boundaries of the law.

The demand for ethical hackers has grown significantly in recent years as organizations recognize the importance of proactive security testing.

Ethical hacking plays a critical role in the broader field of cybersecurity by helping organizations identify and address vulnerabilities before they can be exploited by malicious actors.

Ethical hackers, also known as "penetration testers" or "white hat" hackers, are highly skilled individuals with in-depth knowledge of computer systems, networks, and cybersecurity.

They are often certified in various cybersecurity certifications such as Certified Ethical Hacker (CEH) or Offensive Security Certified Professional (OSCP).

Ethical hackers use a range of tools and methodologies to simulate real-world cyberattacks, testing the defenses of an organization's digital assets.

These tests encompass a variety of areas, including network security, application security, and physical security.

One of the fundamental activities of ethical hacking is network penetration testing.

In this process, ethical hackers attempt to identify vulnerabilities in an organization's network infrastructure.

They use scanning tools like Nmap and Nessus to discover open ports, services, and potential entry points into the network.

Once vulnerabilities are identified, ethical hackers assess their severity and potential impact on the organization.

Web application penetration testing is another critical aspect of ethical hacking, focusing on identifying vulnerabilities in web applications and websites.

Tools like Burp Suite and OWASP ZAP help ethical hackers test for issues such as SQL injection, cross-site scripting (XSS), and insecure authentication mechanisms.

These vulnerabilities, if left unaddressed, can lead to data breaches and other security incidents.

Mobile application penetration testing is also essential as the use of mobile apps continues to rise.

Ethical hackers use tools like MobSF and APKTool to analyze mobile apps for security flaws that could compromise user data and privacy.

This testing ensures that organizations can protect their users from potential threats associated with mobile applications.

Social engineering testing is yet another critical facet of ethical hacking, involving attempts to manipulate individuals into revealing confidential information or performing actions that could compromise security.

Phishing, pretexting, and baiting are common social engineering techniques that ethical hackers use to assess an organization's susceptibility to such attacks.

By conducting social engineering tests, organizations can educate employees and strengthen their awareness of potential threats.

Physical security testing is an often-overlooked aspect of ethical hacking, yet it is crucial for assessing the security of an organization's physical premises.

Ethical hackers may attempt to gain unauthorized access to buildings, server rooms, or data centers to evaluate the effectiveness of physical security measures.

This type of testing helps organizations prevent unauthorized personnel from physically compromising their infrastructure.

In addition to these specific testing areas, ethical hackers also engage in wireless network penetration testing.

They use tools like Aircrack-ng and Wireshark to assess the security of Wi-Fi networks, including the strength of encryption protocols like WPA and WPA2.

This ensures that unauthorized individuals cannot gain unauthorized access to the network.

Throughout the ethical hacking process, careful documentation is essential.

Ethical hackers maintain detailed records of their findings, including the vulnerabilities discovered, their severity, and recommended remediation steps.

This documentation is then presented to the organization's security team, along with recommendations for improving security measures.

Ethical hackers must maintain a high level of professionalism and integrity throughout their engagements.

They operate with the explicit permission of the organization being tested and adhere to a strict code of ethics to ensure their activities remain lawful and ethical.

The ethical hacking process is a continuous cycle of testing, analysis, and improvement.

After identifying vulnerabilities and weaknesses, ethical hackers work with organizations to implement security enhancements and monitor the effectiveness of these measures.

This iterative process helps organizations stay ahead of emerging cyber threats and continuously improve their security posture.

Ethical hacking is not a one-time event but an ongoing commitment to safeguarding digital assets and data.

In summary, ethical hacking for defensive purposes is a vital practice in today's cybersecurity landscape.

Ethical hackers play a crucial role in identifying and mitigating vulnerabilities before malicious actors can exploit them.

Their expertise and ethical approach help organizations strengthen their security defenses, protect sensitive data, and maintain the trust of their customers and stakeholders.

As the cybersecurity landscape continues to evolve, ethical hacking remains a cornerstone of proactive security measures to combat cyber threats effectively.

Chapter 7: Enterprise-Level Security Strategies

Security strategies for large organizations are multifaceted and essential for safeguarding sensitive data and critical assets.

Large organizations face unique challenges due to their size, complexity, and the vast amount of data they handle.

These challenges require comprehensive and tailored security measures to mitigate risks effectively.

One of the primary components of security strategies for large organizations is risk assessment.

Understanding the specific risks that the organization faces is crucial for prioritizing security measures.

Risk assessments consider factors like the organization's industry, regulatory requirements, and the types of data it processes.

By identifying potential vulnerabilities and threats, organizations can create a more targeted and effective security strategy.

Access control is another critical aspect of security for large organizations.

Implementing robust access control mechanisms ensures that only authorized individuals can access sensitive systems and data.

Role-based access control (RBAC) is commonly used to assign permissions based on job roles, limiting access to only what is necessary for employees to perform their duties.

Multi-factor authentication (MFA) adds an extra layer of security by requiring users to provide multiple forms of verification before granting access.

Network security is paramount for large organizations with extensive IT infrastructure.

Implementing firewalls, intrusion detection systems (IDS), and intrusion prevention systems (IPS) helps protect the network from unauthorized access and potential cyber threats.

Network segmentation is also crucial, dividing the network into smaller, isolated segments to contain breaches and limit lateral movement by attackers.

Encryption is a fundamental security measure for protecting sensitive data both in transit and at rest.

Large organizations should encrypt data using strong encryption algorithms, ensuring that even if data is compromised, it remains unreadable without the appropriate decryption keys.

Data loss prevention (DLP) solutions can help monitor and control the flow of sensitive data within the organization, preventing accidental or malicious leaks.

Large organizations often deal with extensive amounts of data, making data backup and recovery crucial.

Regular backups ensure that data can be restored in the event of data loss due to hardware failures, cyberattacks, or human errors.

Large organizations may consider both on-site and off-site backup solutions to enhance data resilience.

Endpoint security is another critical area for large organizations, as employees use various devices to access company resources.

Endpoint security solutions, such as antivirus software, endpoint detection and response (EDR) systems, and mobile device management (MDM) tools, help protect devices from malware and unauthorized access.

Large organizations often manage multiple cloud environments and services, making cloud security essential.

Implementing robust identity and access management (IAM) controls ensures that only authorized individuals can access cloud resources.

Regularly monitoring cloud environments for security threats and misconfigurations helps prevent data breaches.

Security information and event management (SIEM) systems are essential for large organizations to monitor and analyze security events across the enterprise.

SIEM tools aggregate and correlate data from various sources, allowing security teams to detect and respond to security incidents more effectively.

Incident response plans are crucial for large organizations to handle security incidents promptly and efficiently.

These plans outline the steps to take in the event of a security breach, including communication, investigation, and remediation.

Regularly testing and updating incident response plans is essential to ensure they remain effective.

Employee training and awareness programs are vital components of security strategies for large organizations.

Educating employees about security best practices, social engineering tactics, and the importance of data protection helps create a security-conscious workforce.

Regular security awareness training reinforces these principles and ensures that employees stay informed about evolving threats.

Compliance with industry regulations and standards is often a requirement for large organizations.

Maintaining compliance helps avoid legal and financial penalties while also demonstrating a commitment to security and data privacy.

Security audits and assessments play a crucial role in evaluating the effectiveness of security measures.

Regularly conducting security audits and assessments can identify weaknesses and gaps in security controls, allowing organizations to address them promptly.

Large organizations should also consider threat intelligence feeds to stay informed about emerging cyber threats and vulnerabilities relevant to their industry.

Integrating threat intelligence into their security operations helps security teams proactively defend against potential attacks.

Vendor risk management is essential for organizations that rely on third-party vendors and service providers.

Assessing and monitoring the security practices of vendors helps ensure that they meet the organization's security standards and do not introduce risks.

Security incident reporting and communication protocols are crucial for large organizations.

Clear communication channels ensure that security incidents are reported promptly and escalated as needed to contain and mitigate the impact.

Regular security drills and tabletop exercises help organizations test their incident response plans and improve coordination among security teams.

In summary, security strategies for large organizations encompass a wide range of measures and practices.

Risk assessment, access control, network security, encryption, data backup, endpoint security, cloud security, and incident response are all essential components.

Employee training, compliance, security audits, threat intelligence, vendor risk management, and incident reporting are also crucial aspects of a comprehensive security strategy.

By addressing these areas and continually adapting to evolving threats, large organizations can protect their assets, data, and reputation in an increasingly complex cybersecurity landscape.

Scaling security measures for enterprises is a complex and multifaceted task that requires a comprehensive approach to protect against evolving cyber threats.

Enterprises, by their very nature, are large and diverse organizations with extensive digital footprints, making them attractive targets for cybercriminals.

To effectively scale security measures, enterprises must consider a wide range of factors, including their size, industry, regulatory requirements, and the criticality of their data and systems.

One of the key challenges in scaling security for enterprises is managing the sheer volume of devices, applications, and data that need protection.

Enterprises often have thousands or even millions of endpoints, ranging from employee workstations and mobile devices to servers and IoT devices.

Implementing robust endpoint security solutions is critical to defend against malware, phishing attacks, and other threats that can compromise these endpoints.

Enterprises must also consider the complexity of their networks, which can span multiple locations, data centers, and cloud environments.

Network security measures, such as firewalls, intrusion detection and prevention systems (IDPS), and network segmentation, are essential to safeguarding against unauthorized access and lateral movement by attackers.

Data security is a paramount concern for enterprises, especially those that handle sensitive customer information or proprietary data.

Encrypting data at rest and in transit, implementing data loss prevention (DLP) solutions, and enforcing access controls are critical components of a data-centric security strategy.

Identity and access management (IAM) is crucial for enterprises to ensure that only authorized individuals have access to their systems and resources.

IAM solutions help manage user identities, assign access privileges, and enforce strong authentication mechanisms, such as multi-factor authentication (MFA).

Enterprises often rely on cloud services and infrastructure to scale their operations, introducing cloud security considerations.

Securing cloud environments requires a combination of robust IAM controls, data encryption, and continuous monitoring to detect and respond to security incidents.

Compliance with industry regulations and standards is a significant concern for many enterprises.

Meeting regulatory requirements, such as GDPR, HIPAA, or PCI DSS, is essential to avoid legal and financial penalties.

Security awareness and training programs are vital to educate employees about security best practices and the potential risks they may encounter.

Regular training helps foster a security-conscious culture within the enterprise, reducing the likelihood of security incidents caused by human error.

Incident response planning and testing are crucial for enterprises to effectively respond to security breaches.

Creating an incident response plan, establishing communication channels, and conducting tabletop exercises can help the organization respond swiftly and minimize the impact of security incidents.

Enterprise security operations centers (SOCs) play a central role in monitoring, detecting, and responding to security threats.

SOCs use security information and event management (SIEM) systems, threat intelligence feeds, and skilled analysts to identify and mitigate security incidents.

Threat intelligence feeds provide enterprises with up-to-date information on emerging threats and vulnerabilities, helping them stay proactive in their defense.

Security audits and assessments are essential for evaluating the effectiveness of security measures and identifying areas that need improvement.

Regular audits can help enterprises stay ahead of evolving threats and ensure that their security posture remains robust.

Third-party risk management is critical for enterprises that rely on vendors and service providers.

Assessing the security practices of third parties ensures that they meet the organization's security standards and do not introduce risks.

Security automation and orchestration can help enterprises scale their security measures by automating routine tasks, such as threat detection and response.

Automation enables faster response times and reduces the workload on security teams, allowing them to focus on more complex tasks.

Large enterprises often face targeted attacks from sophisticated adversaries.

Advanced threat detection technologies, such as behavior-based analytics and machine learning, are essential for identifying and mitigating advanced threats.

Enterprise security strategies should also consider the evolving threat landscape, which includes new attack vectors and techniques.

Security teams must stay vigilant and adapt their defenses to address emerging threats.

In summary, scaling security measures for enterprises is a multifaceted challenge that requires a holistic approach.

Factors such as the size of the organization, the complexity of its network, the sensitivity of its data, and industry-specific regulations all influence the security strategy.

A combination of endpoint security, network security, data security, IAM, cloud security, compliance, training, incident response, SOCs, threat intelligence, audits, third-party risk management, automation, and advanced threat detection is necessary to protect large enterprises against a constantly evolving threat landscape.

Chapter 8: Securing IoT Devices and Smart Technologies

In the ever-expanding landscape of the Internet of Things (IoT), security challenges loom large, demanding innovative solutions to protect connected devices and networks.

IoT security challenges arise from the sheer scale and diversity of IoT devices, ranging from smart thermostats and wearable fitness trackers to industrial sensors and autonomous vehicles.

One of the foremost challenges is the proliferation of vulnerable devices with limited security capabilities, making them attractive targets for cyberattacks.

These devices often lack sufficient computing power, memory, or security features to withstand sophisticated threats.

IoT devices frequently rely on default usernames and passwords, making them susceptible to brute-force attacks and unauthorized access.

To address this challenge, manufacturers must implement strong password policies, encourage users to change default credentials, and consider using unique device identifiers instead of generic usernames.

Another security challenge is the lack of regular updates and patch management for IoT devices.

Many IoT manufacturers do not provide consistent software updates, leaving devices exposed to known vulnerabilities.

Solutions involve establishing industry standards for firmware updates and creating mechanisms for users to easily apply patches to their devices.

Interoperability and standardization in the IoT ecosystem present challenges, as devices from different manufacturers often use proprietary protocols and communication methods.

To overcome this, industry organizations are working to define common standards for IoT communication and data exchange, enabling devices to work seamlessly together.

The massive amount of data generated by IoT devices also poses security and privacy concerns.

IoT devices collect and transmit data about user behavior, location, and preferences, raising questions about data ownership, consent, and protection.

Privacy-by-design principles and data anonymization techniques can help mitigate these challenges, allowing users to maintain control over their data.

IoT networks are susceptible to various types of attacks, such as Distributed Denial of Service (DDoS) attacks that can disrupt the functioning of connected devices.

To combat this, network security solutions, including intrusion detection systems (IDS) and firewalls, are essential to detect and block malicious traffic.

Securing the communication between IoT devices and backend servers is another challenge, as data transmitted over the internet can be intercepted or tampered with.

Implementing secure communication protocols, such as Transport Layer Security (TLS), can ensure the confidentiality and integrity of data in transit.

Inadequate physical security measures for IoT devices can also pose risks, especially in critical infrastructure and healthcare settings.

Solutions involve implementing tamper-resistant hardware, access controls, and physical security best practices to protect IoT devices from physical attacks.

IoT security challenges extend to supply chain risks, as malicious actors may compromise devices during the manufacturing or distribution process.

IoT manufacturers must establish secure supply chain practices to minimize the risk of tampering and ensure the integrity of their devices.

The rapid evolution of IoT technologies means that many devices have a limited lifecycle, with some becoming obsolete after a short period.

This poses challenges for long-term security support and necessitates strategies for end-of-life device management, including secure decommissioning and disposal.

Edge computing, where data processing occurs closer to the source of data generation, is gaining prominence in IoT deployments.

While edge computing can enhance efficiency and reduce latency, it also introduces security challenges, such as securing edge devices and ensuring data integrity at the edge.

Solutions involve implementing security measures specifically designed for edge environments, including edge gateways and access controls.

As IoT devices often operate in resource-constrained environments, traditional security solutions may not be suitable.

Low-power and lightweight security protocols are essential to ensure that security does not compromise device performance and battery life.

Machine learning and artificial intelligence (AI) are increasingly being used to enhance IoT security by detecting anomalous behavior and identifying potential threats.

These technologies can analyze vast amounts of data generated by IoT devices to detect patterns indicative of security breaches.

To address IoT security challenges effectively, collaboration among stakeholders, including manufacturers, regulatory bodies, and security experts, is essential.

Creating a cybersecurity framework for IoT, setting security standards, and sharing threat intelligence can help establish a robust security ecosystem.

Continuous monitoring and incident response capabilities are crucial for quickly identifying and mitigating security breaches in IoT environments.

Establishing Security Operations Centers (SOCs) specifically tailored for IoT can enhance threat detection and response capabilities.

In summary, IoT security challenges are complex and multifaceted, stemming from the diversity of devices, data, and ecosystems.

Solutions involve improving device security, standardizing communication protocols, addressing data privacy concerns, enhancing network security, and considering edge computing security.

The ongoing collaboration among stakeholders and the implementation of innovative security measures are essential to ensure the continued growth and security of the IoT landscape.

Securing smart devices has become increasingly crucial in today's interconnected world, where everything from household appliances to industrial machinery can be part of the Internet of Things (IoT).

These devices, while convenient and innovative, can also introduce significant security risks if not properly protected.

Best practices for securing smart devices start with the recognition that security should be a top priority from the design and development phase.

Manufacturers must follow security-by-design principles, integrating security features and controls into the devices' architecture.

A crucial aspect of securing smart devices is ensuring that they receive regular software updates and patches.

This helps address known vulnerabilities and ensures that the devices remain resilient to emerging threats.

Manufacturers should establish mechanisms for automatic updates or provide clear instructions to users on how to apply patches.

Implementing strong authentication mechanisms is essential for controlling access to smart devices.

Passwords should be complex, unique, and regularly changed, and two-factor authentication (2FA) should be encouraged or enforced whenever possible.

Network security plays a critical role in safeguarding smart devices.

It is recommended to segment IoT devices onto a separate network to prevent potential compromise from affecting the primary network.

Firewalls and intrusion detection systems (IDS) can provide an additional layer of protection.

Securing communication between smart devices and the cloud or other services is vital.

Encryption protocols, such as TLS (Transport Layer Security), should be used to ensure the confidentiality and integrity of data in transit.

For remote access to devices, Virtual Private Networks (VPNs) or secure remote access solutions should be employed.

Smart devices should have robust access controls in place to limit the number of users and the level of access they have.

Each user should have a unique account with appropriate permissions.

Manufacturers should also provide users with the ability to revoke access to devices and services as needed.

Device identity and integrity checks should be implemented to verify that the device has not been tampered with or compromised.

This can include secure boot processes and code signing to ensure the authenticity of device firmware and software.

Regular security audits and vulnerability assessments should be conducted to identify and address potential weaknesses in the device's security posture.

This proactive approach helps in detecting and mitigating vulnerabilities before they can be exploited.

Data protection and privacy are paramount when dealing with smart devices that collect and transmit user data.

Manufacturers should clearly communicate their data collection and usage policies to users and obtain explicit consent.

Data should be anonymized and stored securely, with access restricted to authorized personnel only.

User awareness and education are crucial aspects of securing smart devices.

Manufacturers should provide clear instructions on how to configure and use devices securely.

Users should be educated about the potential risks and encouraged to take security precautions.

Regularly monitoring device behavior for signs of anomalies or unauthorized access can help detect security breaches early.

This can be achieved through the use of intrusion detection systems, security monitoring tools, or security operations centers (SOCs).

For enterprises and organizations deploying smart devices, it is essential to have a comprehensive IoT security policy in place.

This policy should outline security requirements, procedures, and responsibilities, ensuring that all stakeholders are aware of their roles in securing devices.

Furthermore, organizations should conduct risk assessments to identify potential threats and vulnerabilities specific to their IoT deployments.

Contingency plans and incident response procedures should be established to handle security incidents swiftly and effectively.

Regularly updating and maintaining an inventory of all deployed smart devices is crucial for tracking their lifecycle, including end-of-life considerations.

Devices that are no longer supported or updated should be replaced or taken out of service.

Securing smart devices also requires manufacturers to have a clear and transparent approach to handling security incidents and vulnerabilities.

This includes providing a way for users to report security issues, a process for investigating and addressing them, and timely disclosure of any breaches or vulnerabilities.

Third-party security assessments and certifications can provide additional assurance of a device's security.

Manufacturers should consider undergoing security audits by independent organizations to validate their security claims.

Lastly, collaboration within the industry and sharing threat intelligence can help enhance the security of smart devices collectively.

Manufacturers, researchers, and security experts should work together to identify emerging threats and develop countermeasures.

In summary, best practices for securing smart devices encompass a holistic approach that begins with secure design principles, continues with regular updates and patches, and includes strong authentication, network security, and encryption.

Access controls, identity checks, security audits, and user education are also vital components of device security.

For organizations, a well-defined IoT security policy, risk assessment, and incident response plan are essential.

Transparency, third-party assessments, and industry collaboration further contribute to the overall security of smart devices.

Chapter 9: Privacy and Data Protection in the Digital Age

In today's digital age, data privacy has become a paramount concern for individuals, organizations, and governments around the world.

The increasing volume of personal data being collected, processed, and shared has raised important questions about how that data is handled and protected.

As a response to these concerns, data privacy regulations have emerged as a critical aspect of the modern legal and regulatory landscape.

One of the most notable data privacy regulations is the European Union's General Data Protection Regulation (GDPR), which came into effect in May 2018.

The GDPR applies to any organization that processes the personal data of EU residents, regardless of where the organization is located.

It imposes strict requirements on how personal data is collected, processed, and stored, and grants individuals greater control over their data.

Key principles of the GDPR include transparency, consent, and the right to access and erase one's own data.

To comply with the GDPR, organizations must appoint a Data Protection Officer (DPO), conduct Data Protection Impact Assessments (DPIAs), and report data breaches within 72 hours.

Another significant data privacy regulation is the California Consumer Privacy Act (CCPA), which went into effect on January 1, 2020.

The CCPA grants California residents the right to know what personal information is collected about them, the right to delete their data, and the right to opt-out of the sale of their data.

Organizations subject to the CCPA must provide clear and accessible privacy notices, as well as mechanisms for consumers to exercise their rights.

The regulation applies to businesses that meet certain criteria, including having annual gross revenues exceeding $25 million or handling the personal information of 50,000 or more California residents.

Beyond the GDPR and CCPA, numerous other data privacy regulations exist at the national, regional, and industry levels.

For example, the Health Insurance Portability and Accountability Act (HIPAA) in the United States sets strict standards for the protection of healthcare-related data.

Similarly, the Payment Card Industry Data Security Standard (PCI DSS) mandates security measures for organizations that handle payment card data.

Data privacy regulations serve several essential purposes in today's digital landscape.

First and foremost, they aim to protect individuals' privacy rights by defining how their personal data can be collected, processed, and used.

These regulations also foster transparency and accountability within organizations by requiring them to disclose their data handling practices and appoint responsible data protection officers.

Moreover, data privacy regulations encourage organizations to implement robust security measures to safeguard sensitive data from breaches and unauthorized access.

Non-compliance with data privacy regulations can result in severe consequences, including hefty fines, legal actions, and damage to an organization's reputation.

For example, the GDPR empowers supervisory authorities to impose fines of up to €20 million or 4% of the organization's global annual revenue, whichever is higher.

The CCPA allows for statutory damages ranging from $100 to $750 per California resident for certain data breaches.

To achieve compliance with data privacy regulations, organizations must take several steps.

First, they need to understand the specific requirements of the relevant regulations that apply to their operations.

This involves conducting a thorough data inventory to identify what personal data is collected, where it is stored, and how it is processed.

Organizations must then implement data protection policies and procedures that align with the regulations' principles and requirements.

This includes establishing data retention policies, data breach response plans, and mechanisms for obtaining consent from data subjects.

Privacy notices and consent forms should be clear, concise, and easily accessible to individuals.

Additionally, organizations should provide training and awareness programs to educate employees about data privacy and security best practices.

Data encryption, access controls, and regular security audits are essential components of a comprehensive data protection strategy.

Furthermore, organizations should appoint a Data Protection Officer (DPO) or a responsible individual to oversee data privacy compliance efforts.

The DPO's role includes monitoring data processing activities, responding to data subject requests, and serving as a point of contact for supervisory authorities.

Regular audits and assessments of data processing activities can help organizations identify and rectify compliance gaps.

It's crucial for organizations to establish a process for reporting data breaches promptly and effectively.

Under many data privacy regulations, data breaches must be reported to supervisory authorities and affected data subjects within a specified timeframe.

Organizations should also have a plan in place to mitigate the impact of breaches and prevent further unauthorized access.

In summary, data privacy regulations have become a central concern in today's digital world, with the GDPR, CCPA, and numerous other regulations shaping how organizations handle personal data.

Compliance with these regulations is not only a legal requirement but also a critical aspect of protecting individuals' privacy rights and maintaining trust in the digital ecosystem.

To achieve compliance, organizations must understand the specific requirements of relevant regulations, implement data protection policies and procedures, educate employees, and establish robust security measures.

Data privacy is an ongoing effort that requires continuous monitoring and adaptation to evolving regulatory landscapes and emerging threats. In today's interconnected and data-driven world, data protection has become a critical concern for individuals and organizations alike. The rapid digitization of information has led to the creation, transmission, and storage of vast amounts of data, including personal and sensitive information. As a result, the need for robust data protection strategies has never been greater.

Data protection encompasses a wide range of practices, technologies, and policies designed to safeguard data from unauthorized access, theft, or loss.

The importance of data protection is underscored by the potential consequences of data breaches, which can include financial loss, reputational damage, and legal liabilities.

One of the key elements of modern data protection strategies is encryption.

Encryption is the process of encoding data in a way that makes it unreadable to anyone without the appropriate decryption key.

It is an effective method for ensuring the confidentiality of sensitive information, whether it's stored on a device, transmitted over a network, or stored in the cloud.

End-to-end encryption, for example, ensures that only the sender and intended recipient can decipher the contents of a message or file.

Encryption is a fundamental tool in data protection because it safeguards information from unauthorized access, even if a breach occurs.

Another crucial aspect of data protection is access control.

Access control mechanisms determine who can access data, what actions they can perform, and under what circumstances.

Role-based access control (RBAC) and discretionary access control (DAC) are common methods used to manage and restrict data access.

RBAC assigns permissions based on predefined roles within an organization, ensuring that individuals have the appropriate level of access for their job responsibilities.

DAC, on the other hand, allows data owners to specify access permissions for specific users or groups.

Access control extends beyond internal personnel and includes external parties such as customers, partners, and vendors.

Implementing strong authentication methods, such as multi-factor authentication (MFA), adds an extra layer of security to ensure that only authorized individuals can access sensitive data.

Data protection also involves data classification and labeling.

Data classification categorizes information based on its sensitivity, importance, and regulatory requirements.

Once data is classified, organizations can apply appropriate security controls and policies to protect it.

For instance, highly sensitive financial data may require stricter encryption and access controls than less critical information.

Data labeling involves clearly marking data to indicate its classification and any associated restrictions.

This helps users and systems identify how data should be handled and protected.

Data protection extends to data in transit and data at rest.

Data in transit refers to information that is being transmitted over a network or between systems.

Encrypting data in transit ensures that it remains secure while moving from one location to another.

This is especially important for sensitive communications, such as online banking transactions or healthcare data exchanges.

Data at rest refers to information that is stored on devices, servers, or in databases.

Securing data at rest involves measures such as full-disk encryption, database encryption, and secure storage solutions.

Regular data backups and disaster recovery plans are also vital components of data protection strategies.

In the event of data loss due to hardware failure, cyberattacks, or natural disasters, having backup copies of data ensures that it can be recovered and restored.

Backup solutions should include redundancy and off-site storage to minimize the risk of data loss.

Data protection also involves data retention and disposal policies.

Organizations must define how long data should be retained based on legal requirements, business needs, and data classification.

Once data reaches the end of its lifecycle, it should be securely disposed of to prevent unauthorized access or recovery.

This may involve shredding physical documents or securely erasing digital data.

Data protection is closely tied to compliance with data privacy regulations.

Regulations such as the General Data Protection Regulation (GDPR) in the European Union and the California Consumer Privacy Act (CCPA) impose strict requirements on how organizations handle and protect personal data.

Non-compliance with these regulations can result in significant fines and legal consequences.

To ensure compliance, organizations must conduct privacy impact assessments, provide individuals with transparent privacy notices, and obtain explicit consent for data processing when required.

Data protection strategies also encompass monitoring and auditing data access and usage.

Regularly reviewing logs and audit trails helps detect suspicious or unauthorized activities.

Security information and event management (SIEM) systems can assist in real-time monitoring and alerting.

Security policies and procedures, as well as employee training, play a crucial role in data protection.

Employees need to be aware of security best practices, recognize phishing attempts, and understand their role in safeguarding data.

To create a culture of data protection, organizations should establish clear policies for data handling, incident reporting, and security awareness.

In summary, data protection strategies for the modern era are multifaceted and essential for safeguarding sensitive information in an increasingly interconnected world.

Encryption, access control, data classification, and secure storage are fundamental components of data protection.

Compliance with data privacy regulations, such as GDPR and CCPA, is also critical to avoid legal repercussions.

Regular monitoring, auditing, and employee training are integral to maintaining robust data protection practices.

In an age where data is a valuable asset and a target for cyber threats, organizations must prioritize data protection as a fundamental aspect of their operations.

Chapter 10: Navigating the Legal and Ethical Aspects of Cybersecurity

Legal frameworks in cybersecurity provide the foundation for addressing digital threats and protecting critical infrastructure in the digital age.

These frameworks encompass a complex web of laws, regulations, and international agreements that aim to establish rules and responsibilities for various stakeholders in the cybersecurity ecosystem.

One of the primary objectives of these legal frameworks is to define and clarify the rights and obligations of individuals, organizations, and governments in the context of cybersecurity.

At the international level, organizations such as the United Nations and INTERPOL have taken steps to promote global cooperation in combating cybercrime.

The Budapest Convention on Cybercrime, for example, is an international treaty that addresses computer-related offenses and facilitates cross-border cooperation in cybercrime investigations.

While international agreements are essential for addressing cyber threats that transcend borders, individual countries have also developed their own cybersecurity laws and regulations.

These national frameworks vary widely in scope and focus but generally aim to safeguard critical infrastructure, protect personal data, and combat cybercrime.

In the United States, for instance, the Cybersecurity Information Sharing Act (CISA) encourages the sharing of cybersecurity threat information between the government and private sector entities.

The European Union has enacted the General Data Protection Regulation (GDPR), which governs the processing of personal data and imposes strict data protection requirements on organizations.

Another key aspect of legal frameworks in cybersecurity is the establishment of regulatory authorities and enforcement mechanisms.

These authorities are responsible for overseeing compliance with cybersecurity laws and regulations and may have the power to investigate breaches and impose sanctions.

The Federal Trade Commission (FTC) in the United States, for example, has the authority to take enforcement action against organizations that fail to protect consumer data adequately.

In addition to national laws and regulations, many industries have their own cybersecurity standards and guidelines.

For example, the Payment Card Industry Data Security Standard (PCI DSS) sets security requirements for organizations that handle payment card data.

These industry-specific standards often complement and align with broader legal frameworks.

Legal frameworks also play a crucial role in addressing cybersecurity incidents and data breaches.

They establish notification requirements for organizations that experience a breach, specifying when and how affected individuals and regulatory authorities should be informed.

Failure to comply with these notification requirements can result in significant penalties and legal consequences.

Moreover, legal frameworks provide a basis for holding individuals and organizations accountable for cybercrimes.

Cybercriminals can be prosecuted and brought to justice under the laws of the countries in which their actions have caused harm.

Extradition agreements and international legal cooperation mechanisms are essential for ensuring that cybercriminals cannot evade justice by crossing borders.

Furthermore, legal frameworks address liability and responsibility in cybersecurity.

They define the legal obligations of organizations to protect data and systems and establish liability for failures to do so.

This includes potential liability for damages incurred by individuals or entities affected by a cyber incident.

Legal frameworks also address the protection of critical infrastructure, such as energy grids, transportation systems, and financial institutions.

Governments often designate certain sectors as critical infrastructure and impose specific cybersecurity requirements on them. These requirements may include mandatory cybersecurity standards, information sharing agreements, and incident reporting obligations.

International norms and principles play a significant role in shaping legal frameworks in cybersecurity.

Cybersecurity experts, legal scholars, and governments have engaged in discussions on responsible state behavior in cyberspace.

Efforts such as the Tallinn Manual and the United Nations Group of Governmental Experts (UN GGE) have contributed to the development of norms governing state conduct in cyberspace.

These norms emphasize the prohibition of cyberattacks on critical infrastructure, the protection of civilian infrastructure, and the responsibility of states to prevent cybercrime.

Moreover, legal frameworks address issues related to surveillance and privacy in the digital age.

They define the conditions under which governments can conduct surveillance on individuals and collect electronic evidence.

These conditions often require compliance with due process, judicial oversight, and protection of individuals' privacy rights.

The tension between national security concerns and individual privacy rights is a recurring theme in discussions about legal frameworks in cybersecurity.

Cybersecurity laws and regulations are continuously evolving to keep pace with the ever-changing threat landscape.

New technologies, such as artificial intelligence and quantum computing, present both opportunities and challenges in the realm of cybersecurity.

As such, legal frameworks must adapt to address emerging threats and vulnerabilities.

Additionally, international cooperation remains crucial in addressing global cybersecurity challenges.

Efforts to develop and harmonize international norms and standards will play a significant role in shaping the future of legal frameworks in cybersecurity.

In summary, legal frameworks in cybersecurity are essential for establishing rules and responsibilities in the digital age.

They encompass a complex web of laws, regulations, and international agreements that define rights, obligations, and enforcement mechanisms.

These frameworks address issues such as data protection, critical infrastructure, incident response, and accountability for cybercrimes.

International norms and principles also shape the development of legal frameworks, emphasizing responsible state behavior and the protection of individual privacy rights.

As technology continues to advance, legal frameworks must adapt to address new challenges and opportunities in the ever-evolving field of cybersecurity. Ethical considerations are at the core of responsible and effective cybersecurity practices, guiding the behavior and decisions of professionals in this field.

In the rapidly evolving landscape of cyberspace, ethical guidelines provide a moral compass to navigate complex challenges and dilemmas. One fundamental ethical principle in cybersecurity is the respect for privacy and individual rights.

Cybersecurity professionals must ensure that their actions and practices do not infringe upon the privacy of individuals or violate their rights.

This includes safeguarding personal data and using it only for legitimate and authorized purposes.

Transparency and informed consent are critical aspects of respecting privacy in the digital age.

Another ethical consideration in cybersecurity is the principle of fairness.

Professionals should ensure that their practices and decisions are fair and impartial, treating all parties equitably.

This is especially important when conducting investigations or responding to incidents, as bias or favoritism can undermine the integrity of the process.

The principle of accountability plays a significant role in ethical cybersecurity practices.

Professionals must take responsibility for their actions and decisions, acknowledging the consequences of their choices.

Accountability also extends to organizations, which should have clear policies and procedures for handling cybersecurity incidents and breaches.

Moreover, ethical considerations require cybersecurity professionals to act with integrity and honesty.

This includes being truthful about the severity of a breach or the effectiveness of security measures, even when the news may be unfavorable.

Integrity also involves avoiding conflicts of interest that could compromise professional judgment.

The principle of security is central to ethical cybersecurity practices.

Professionals have a duty to protect the confidentiality, integrity, and availability of data and systems.

This means implementing robust security measures and staying vigilant against threats and vulnerabilities.

Additionally, ethical cybersecurity professionals should continuously update their knowledge and skills to stay current with evolving threats and technologies.

Ethical guidelines also emphasize the importance of collaboration and cooperation.

Professionals should work together with colleagues, other organizations, and law enforcement agencies to combat cyber threats effectively.

Sharing threat intelligence and best practices can enhance the collective security of the digital ecosystem.

Ethical cybersecurity practices extend beyond technical expertise to encompass social responsibility.

Professionals should be aware of the broader societal implications of their work, considering the potential impact on individuals, communities, and nations.

For example, the development of cyber weapons or offensive capabilities should be approached with caution and a strong ethical framework.

Another ethical consideration relates to the disclosure of vulnerabilities.

Cybersecurity researchers and professionals often discover vulnerabilities in software or systems.

Ethical guidelines emphasize responsible disclosure, which involves notifying the affected parties, including vendors or developers, before making vulnerabilities public.

This approach allows time for patches or fixes to be developed, minimizing the risk to users.

When it comes to ethical dilemmas in cybersecurity, professionals may encounter situations where the right course of action is not immediately clear.

In such cases, seeking guidance from colleagues, mentors, or professional organizations can be helpful.

Ethical codes of conduct and professional associations often provide valuable resources and support in navigating complex ethical challenges.

One common ethical dilemma involves balancing the need for security with the right to privacy.

Cybersecurity measures, such as surveillance or data collection, may be necessary for protecting against threats, but they can also raise concerns about privacy infringement.

In such cases, ethical professionals should carefully weigh the risks and benefits and consider less invasive alternatives.

The ethical use of artificial intelligence (AI) and machine learning (ML) in cybersecurity is another evolving challenge.

AI and ML technologies can enhance threat detection and response, but they also raise questions about bias, transparency, and accountability.

Ethical guidelines emphasize the responsible development and deployment of AI and ML in cybersecurity.

The concept of "hacktivism" presents yet another ethical dilemma.

Some individuals or groups engage in hacking activities for political, social, or ideological reasons.

Ethical cybersecurity professionals should refrain from engaging in illegal or unethical hacktivist activities, even if they align with their personal beliefs.

One overarching ethical principle in cybersecurity is the commitment to the greater good.

Professionals should prioritize the security and well-being of society over personal interests or gains.

This includes reporting illegal activities, cooperating with law enforcement, and advocating for policies that enhance cybersecurity for all.

In summary, ethical considerations are paramount in cybersecurity practices, guiding professionals to act with integrity, fairness, transparency, and accountability.

These principles help ensure the responsible and ethical use of technology in an increasingly interconnected world.

By upholding ethical standards, cybersecurity professionals contribute to a safer and more secure digital environment for individuals, organizations, and society as a whole.

Conclusion

In the pages of "CYBERWATCH 101: THE ART OF CYBER DEFENSE AND INFRASTRUCTURE SECURITY," we embarked on a journey through the ever-evolving landscape of digital security. Through four comprehensive books, we explored the spectrum of cybersecurity knowledge, from beginner to expert, uncovering the secrets and strategies to protect our digital world.

In "BOOK 1 - CYBERWATCH: A BEGINNER'S GUIDE TO DIGITAL SECURITY," we laid the foundation for understanding the essentials of digital security. We learned to recognize threats, fortify our defenses, and adopt a cybersecurity mindset that empowers us in the digital realm.

"BOOK 2 - MASTERING CYBERWATCH: ADVANCED TECHNIQUES FOR CYBERSECURITY PROFESSIONALS" elevated our expertise, delving into advanced techniques and strategies employed by cybersecurity professionals. We mastered the art of penetration testing, intrusion detection, and advanced encryption, equipping ourselves with the tools needed to stay ahead of sophisticated cyber threats.

"BOOK 3 - CYBERWATCH CHRONICLES: FROM NOVICE TO NINJA IN CYBER DEFENSE" chronicled the journey from novice to ninja, showcasing the evolution of our cyber defense skills. We honed our abilities in network security, incident response, and ethical hacking, transforming into true cybersecurity warriors.

Finally, "BOOK 4 - CYBERWATCH UNLEASHED: EXPERT STRATEGIES FOR SAFEGUARDING YOUR DIGITAL WORLD" unveiled the expert strategies and cutting-edge tactics employed by seasoned cybersecurity experts. We explored advanced cryptographic protocols, secured IoT devices, and navigated the complex legal and ethical aspects of cybersecurity.

As we conclude this bundle, we find ourselves armed with a wealth of knowledge and skills to safeguard our digital existence. The world of cybersecurity is ever-changing, but armed with the insights gained from "CYBERWATCH 101," we are well-prepared to face the challenges that lie ahead. Whether you are a beginner looking to fortify your digital defenses or an expert seeking to stay at the forefront of cybersecurity, this bundle has provided you with the tools and wisdom to succeed in the ever-evolving realm of digital security.

Remember, the journey to cybersecurity mastery is ongoing. Stay vigilant, stay informed, and never stop learning. Your commitment to the art of cyber defense is not only a shield for your digital world but also a beacon of hope in an increasingly interconnected and vulnerable digital landscape. Thank you for joining us on this transformative journey through "CYBERWATCH 101." Your dedication to securing the digital future is our greatest defense.

www.ingramcontent.com/pod-product-compliance
Lightning Source LLC
Chambersburg PA
CBHW071234050326
40690CB00011B/2114